INTROD...

Jung

Maggie Hyde and Michael McGuinness

Edited by Richard Appignanesi

WITHDRAWN

WITHDRAWN

ICON BOOKS UK   TOTEM BOOKS USA

This edition published in the UK
in 1999 by Icon Books Ltd.,
Grange Road, Duxford,
Cambridge CB2 4QF
email: icon@mistral.co.uk
www.iconbooks.co.uk

Distributed in the UK, Europe,
Canada, South Africa and Asia by the
Penguin Group: Penguin Books Ltd.,
27 Wrights Lane, London W8 5TZ

This edition published in Australia
in 1999 by Allen & Unwin Pty. Ltd.,
PO Box 8500, 9 Atchison Street,
St. Leonards NSW 2065

Previously published in the UK and
Australia in 1992 under the title
Jung for Beginners

Reprinted 1993, 1994, 1995, 1996, 1997

First published in the United States
in 1994 by Totem Books
Inquiries to: PO Box 223,
Canal Street Station,
New York, NY 10013

Reprinted 1996, 1997

In the United States,
distributed to the trade by
National Book Network Inc.,
4720 Boston Way, Lanham,
Maryland 20706

Text copyright © 1992 Maggie Hyde
Illustrations copyright © 1992 Michael McGuinness

The author and artist have asserted their moral rights.

Originating editor: Richard Appignanesi

No part of this book may be reproduced in any form, or by any means,
without prior permission in writing from the publisher.

Printed and bound in Australia
by McPherson's Printing Group, Victoria

Boyhood Soul-Searching

Carl Gustav Jung was a strange melancholic child who had no brothers or sisters until he was nine, so he played his own imaginary games.

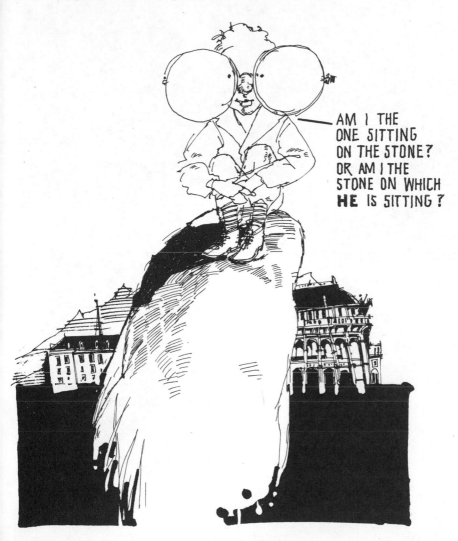

This was his secret stone with a life of **its** own.

He was born 26 July 1875 in Kesswil, Switzerland, the only son of a Swiss Reformed Church Evangelical minister.

The family were steeped in religion. Jung had eight uncles in the clergy, as well as his maternal grandfather. His earliest playgrounds were churches and graveyards. Men in black would bring a black box and talk of "Jesus".

He even heard his father talk of a "Je-suit" (sounds like Je-sus), and that was "something specially dangerous".

THIS JESUS CAN'T BE TRUSTED. HE "TAKES" PEOPLE TO HIMSELF AND THEY'RE PUT IN A HOLE!

4

Jung says that his intellectual life began with a dream at the age of three. In his dream, he descended into a hole in the ground.

It leads him into a large chamber, a red carpet and a golden throne on which a strange being sits.

Decades later, Jung came across a reference to the motif of cannibalism in the symbolism of the Mass. And only then did the image of the "man-eater" make sense to him. He realized that the "dark Lord Jesus, the Jesuit and the phallus were identical". They represented a dark creative force in nature, the investigation of which he pursued throughout his life.

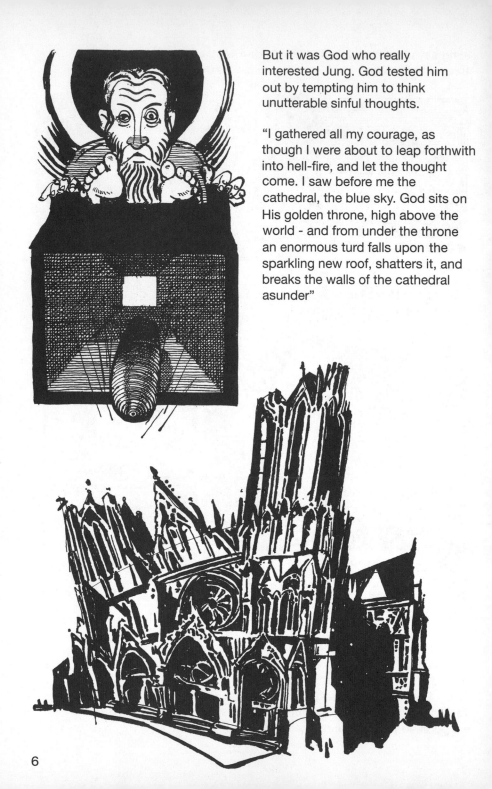

But it was God who really interested Jung. God tested him out by tempting him to think unutterable sinful thoughts.

"I gathered all my courage, as though I were about to leap forthwith into hell-fire, and let the thought come. I saw before me the cathedral, the blue sky. God sits on His golden throne, high above the world - and from under the throne an enormous turd falls upon the sparkling new roof, shatters it, and breaks the walls of the cathedral asunder"

What a relief! Instead of damnation, Jung felt this vision was an act of grace. He had been shown another side of God altogether, different to the one his father and uncles spoke of in their sermons.

BUT WHAT ABOUT THE SECRET? NONE OF YOU KNOW ANYTHING ABOUT THAT. YOU DON'T KNOW THAT GOD WANTS TO FORCE ME TO DO WRONG, TO THINK ABOMINATIONS IN ORDER TO EXPERIENCE HIS GRACE!

Those around him seemed hypocritical and empty. He brooded on the secret, searching in vain in his father's library for more information.

Then he would sit on his stone and it would free him from his turmoils. Jung had a strong suspicion there was something eternal in himself too, some "Other" in him which was like the stone.

IT KNOWS THE SECRET. IT **IS** THE SECRET, BECAUSE IT'S THOUSANDS OF YEARS OLD.

There were other religious influences on Jung, stemming from his mother and maternal grandfather, Samuel Preiswerk, a respected pastor in Basel, who had contact with a different world altogether - the spirit world. Every week he had conversed with his deceased first wife, while his second wife (Jung's grandmother) and his daughter (Jung's mother), listened in.

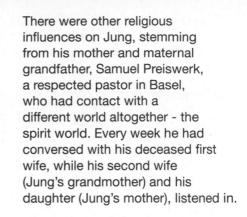

WHILE YOUR GRANDPA WROTE HIS SERMONS, I HAD TO STAND BEHIND HIM TO KEEP THE BAD SPIRITS AWAY.

Contact with the spirits was not unusual amongst Swiss rural folk. Jung experienced his mother as dark and unpredictable, "rooted in deep, invisible ground". She knew the world of the uncanny and she could be frightening and erratic.

These dual religious influences of Swiss Protestantism and pagan spirituality reflected a dualism in Jung himself. He believed he had two different personalities which he named "Number 1" and "Number 2".

Number 1 was involved in the ordinary, everyday world. He could burst into emotions and seemed childish and undisciplined. Yet he was also ambitious for academic success, studying science and aiming to achieve a civilized, prestigious life style.

The Number 2 personality was much more troublesome, the "Other", identified with the stone and the secret of God's grace. Number 2 carried meaning and seemed to stretch back into history in a mysterious manner.

Jung associated his Number 2 dimension with the uncanny world of his mother. He carved a little man wearing a black frock-coat and boots and placed him, with a stone, in a pencil case that he stashed away in a forbidden place in the attic.

In this simple, primitive way, he felt in touch with his Number 2 world.

Years later, Jung recognized that the task of the psychoanalyst was to discover a patient's secret.

Jung's struggle to reconcile his Number 1 and Number 2 worlds persisted throughout adolescence. He recalls his twelfth year when "he learned what a neurosis is". He shirked school with mysterious fainting spells, a "whole bag of tricks" that worried his father.

He conquered his dizzy spells with an effort of will, and had another startling experience around this time. Suddenly, walking along a street, he felt as if he emerged from a wall of mist.

Jung identified more and more with his Number 1 personality and his newly discovered sense of self. The Number 2 world began to slip away. He grew into a tall, handsome, athletic and physically strong young man. Throughout his life these qualities, alongside his loud booming laugh and infectious hearty love of life, gave him tremendous physical presence and enormous charisma, especially with women.

Jung gravitated towards science and philosophy, winning a scholarship to Basel University to study medicine. In his second year, when he was twenty, his father died. The parsonage had to be given up and they moved to Bottminger Mill, near Basel.

I'LL HAVE TO GIVE UP MY STUDIES.

DON'T WORRY. YOUR UNCLE'S LOAN WILL LET YOU CONTINUE.

Jung loved his student days, and alongside medical textbooks he devoured works on philosophy, especially those of Kant and Nietzsche. He also read Swedenborg and studied spiritualism and the paranormal.

Zofingia Days

He became a member of the university debating society, the **Zofingia Club**, formerly an 18th century duelling society. Jung thrived on its intellectual cut and thrust and was able to explore something which held an immense fascination for him - the human Soul.

Kant's ideas about two orientations of the Soul, one towards everyday concerns and the other towards the "spirit" world, echoed Jung's own dualism. If Kant was right, then perhaps paranormal phenomena which distorted time and space could teach us about the Soul. It was therefore essential to investigate parapsychology and such phenomena as hypnosis, spiritualism, clairvoyance and telepathy. What vehicle could he find for such investigations?

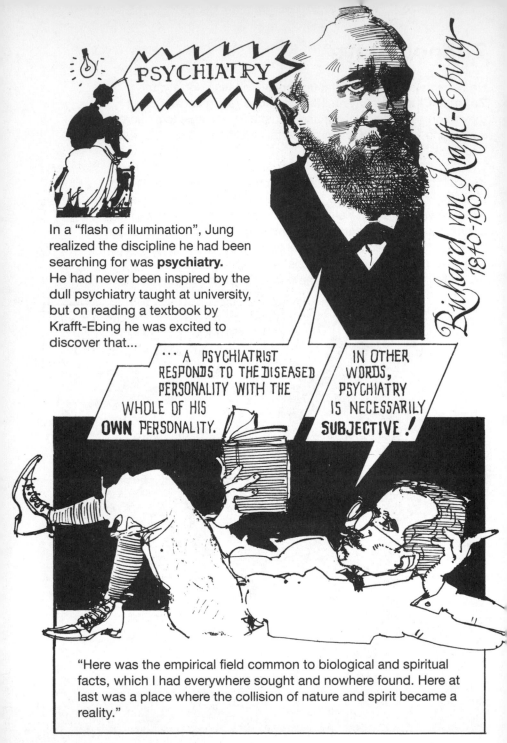

PSYCHIATRY

Richard von Krafft-Ebing 1840-1903

In a "flash of illumination", Jung realized the discipline he had been searching for was **psychiatry.**
He had never been inspired by the dull psychiatry taught at university, but on reading a textbook by Krafft-Ebing he was excited to discover that...

··· A PSYCHIATRIST RESPONDS TO THE DISEASED PERSONALITY WITH THE WHOLE OF HIS **OWN** PERSONALITY.

IN OTHER WORDS, PSYCHIATRY IS NECESSARILY SUBJECTIVE!

"Here was the empirical field common to biological and spiritual facts, which I had everywhere sought and nowhere found. Here at last was a place where the collision of nature and spirit became a reality."

At around the same time, several peculiar incidents happened which confirmed this choice of career in psychiatry. At home with his mother one day, suddenly a"report like a pistol shot" sounded.

MY GOD, OUR OAK TABLE SPLIT RIGHT THROUGH THE CENTRE!

A few weeks later, another "deafening report" was heard coming from a sideboard.

THE STEEL BLADE OF A BREADKNIFE SHATTERED IN PIECES!

THESE OMENS MUST MEAN SOMETHING!

YES, IVE BEEN INVITED TO A **SÉANCE.** THERE'S SOME CONNECTION TO FATHER'S DEATH IN ALL THIS.

Jung attended the séances for over two years. The medium was his fifteen-year-old cousin, Helene Preiswerk, and the deceased Samuel Preiswerk was her spirit guide.

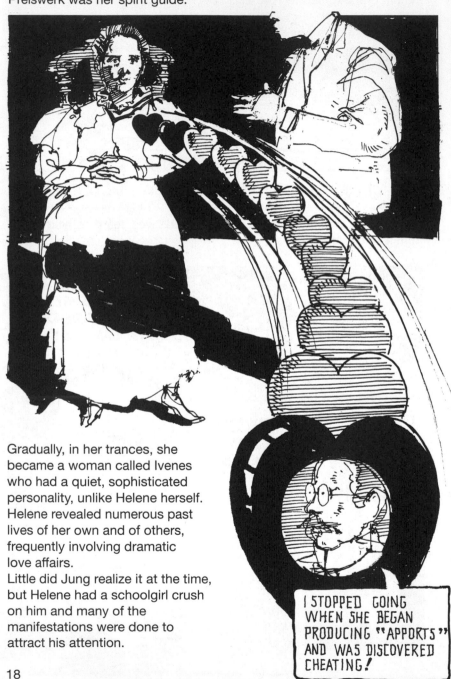

Gradually, in her trances, she became a woman called Ivenes who had a quiet, sophisticated personality, unlike Helene herself. Helene revealed numerous past lives of her own and of others, frequently involving dramatic love affairs.

Little did Jung realize it at the time, but Helene had a schoolgirl crush on him and many of the manifestations were done to attract his attention.

I STOPPED GOING WHEN SHE BEGAN PRODUCING "APPORTS" AND WAS DISCOVERED CHEATING!

Why should these paranormal experiences and séances have anything to do with Jung's choice of psychiatry as a career?

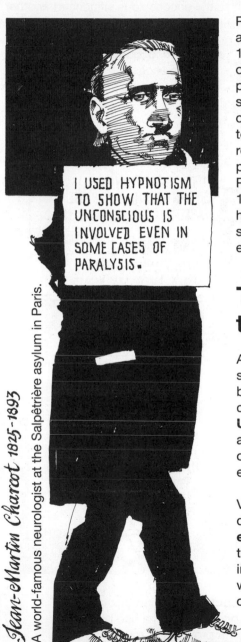

I USED HYPNOTISM TO SHOW THAT THE UNCONSCIOUS IS INVOLVED EVEN IN SOME CASES OF PARALYSIS.

Jean-Martin Charcot 1825-1893 A world-famous neurologist at the Salpêtrière asylum in Paris.

Psychiatry as we know it today was a very different "bag of tricks" in the 1890s when Jung was starting out on his career. Investigation of the psyche (from the Greek, "soul") was seen by many of Jung's contemporaries as intimately related to the problems raised by **psychical** research - the study of "spiritualist" phenomena. The Society for Psychical Research was founded in 1882 to provide evidence that the human psyche was an immaterial substance, not dependent for its existence on the body.

The Discovery of the Unconscious

An understanding of the "twilight states" and the subliminal mind had been developing since the mid-19th century. The existence of the **Unconscious** mind, capable of affecting and interrupting consciousness, was well established.

Various theories concerning the dynamics of **mental** or **psychic energy** explored the possibility that it could become locked in an inaccessible realm of the mind, from whence it could still disrupt consciousness.

19

Freud

Charcot's **materialist** approach to the unconscious influenced another neurologist in the 1880s, Sigmund Freud. Freud's development of **psychoanalysis** had made important inroads into accessing the unconscious, years before Jung met him.

I DROPPED HYPNOSIS AND BEGAN USING A "FREE ASSOCIATION METHOD".

SAYING WHATEVER COMES INTO MY MIND...

THIS METHOD ALLOWS THE PATIENT TO RECALL **FORGOTTEN MEMORIES** ATTACHED TO TRAUMATIC SITUATIONS.

Such recollections were called **abreactive,** meaning that even physical ailments could disappear once the trauma had been recalled. Similarly, symbols in **dreams** provided a "royal road to the unconscious", as did instances of "forgetting" and slips of the tongue.

Freud's non-spiritualist approach to the mysteries of the unconscious mind would have great impact on 20th century psychology. But spiritualism continued to enjoy late 19th century popularity as a valid part of psychology. Jung himself received his training in the materialist school of clinical psychiatry, but he never lost interest in psychical phenomena, and this would lead to trouble with the convinced materialist, Freud, as we'll see later.

THE TROUBLE WAS THAT PSYCHICAL RESEARCH INTO "SPOOKS" HAD MORE CREDIBILITY AND PRESTIGE THAN MY PSYCHOANALYSIS!

Pierre Janet, a disciple of Charcot, investigated the unconscious states of dissociation or "multiple personalities". Working closely with his patient Léonie, he showed that it was the unconscious that spoke during trances.

EITHER BY THE EXPRESSION OF "RESIDUAL MEMORIES" OR SOMETIMES BY TELEPATHY

Pierre Janet 1859-1947

Jung's cousin, the medium Helene Preiswerk, had also created other personalities, especially Ivenes.

Helene's séances presented Jung with a ready-made subject of investigation.

HELENE'S SEANCES BECAME THE SUBJECT OF MY 1902 DOCTORAL THESIS.

HER ACCOMPLISHMENTS AS "IVENES" FAR EXCELLED HER NORMAL CONSCIOUS STATE!

Jung concluded that split-off contents of the unconscious could therefore appear either as another human personality in the form of hallucinations, or they could take control of the conscious mind, as happened during the séances. The unconscious was capable of **compensating** conscious attitudes, which implied that there was an **intentionality** and **purpose** in its creations. Psychic energy thus had a purposeful or **teleological** function.

APPORTS, TELEOLOGICAL ?...THERE'S A LITTLE DICTIONARY AT THE BACK OF THIS BOOK.

Burghölzli

Jung's apprenticeship in psychiatry began in December 1900 when he became an assistant at the Burghölzli Mental Hospital, a clinic attached to the University of Zurich.
All doctors at the Burghölzli had to live in, and it was run like a monastery by its chief, Dr. Eugen Bleuler, one of the most eminent psychiatrists in Switzerland.

AUTHORITARIAN WITH HIS STAFF, BUT KIND AND HUMANE TOWARDS THE MENTALLY ILL.

Jung now encountered at first hand the world of the insane, seeing the inmates as dead souls in the underworld of Hades.

He was faced daily with the tragic plight of mad men and women. These suffered from **psychosis**, an obsession or "unconscious invasion" which had overwhelmed the ordinary mental processes, splitting the individual off from conventional social responses. For nine years at Burghölzli, he took an active part in the pioneering experimental psychology programme run by Bleuler. This focused on the problems of **dementia praecox**, later renamed **schizophrenia** by Bleuler.

THEY DRINK FROM PISS-POTS, SMEAR THEMSELVES WITH SHIT AND SPEAK ONLY GIBBERISH...

WHAT ACTUALLY TAKES PLACE INSIDE THESE HEADS?

Most psychiatrists believed schizophrenia was a degenerative disease of the brain, purely neurological or organic in origin. Bleuler attempted to prevent the disease from becoming chronic by the intensive care of patients during its early stages.
Bleuler achieved many remarkable cures and was also openly sympathetic to Freud's investigations into the unconscious and the psychogenetic formation of mental disturbances.

Under the direction of Bleuler, Jung continued this research and further developed the **word association** tests.

A PATIENT RESPONDS TO A NUMBER OF SPECIALLY SELECTED WORDS WITH THE FIRST ONE THAT COMES TO MIND.

ship
flower
big
to ask

?

The irregularities in the reaction times and word associations were connected with unconscious emotions which clustered to form a **complex**. Jung was able to distinguish different types of complexes and varied origins.

BOTH THE RESPONSE AND REACTION TIME ARE CAREFULLY NOTED.

The Case of Babette

A psychotic patient, an old woman called Babette, fascinated Jung. For twenty years, since the age of thirty-nine, she had been at Burghölzli.

I'M PLUM CAKE ON A CORNMEAL BOTTOM...

NAPLES AND I MUST SUPPLY THE WORLD WITH NOODLES!

When Jung analyzed these expressions through word association, they made sense within the context of her life-story.

Babette's complexes showed a wish to compensate for her feelings of inferiority and her unfortunate life.

SHE WAS BORN IN BACKSTREET MISERY... WITH A DRUNKARD FATHER AND A PROSTITUTE MOTHER.

Psychotic ideas were an individual's attempt to create a new vision of the world.

Jung also experimented with a galvanometer to measure psychological states through skin and sweat gland responses.

NOW THE SO-CALLED " LIE DETECTOR".

He tried to apply the word association test to detect criminals...

... AND CAUGHT A NURSE WHO HAD STOLEN MONEY!

Later, due to Freud's influence, he abandoned this work because he realized that responses depended on an individual's subjective feeling of guilt.

... REGARDLESS OF WHETHER OR NOT HE OR SHE WAS ACTUALLY GUILTY .

Jung's work in these areas gained him recognition, especially in America, and in 1905 he became a senior doctor at Burghölzli and a lecturer in the medical faculty of the University of Zurich. Yet as he discovered more about psychoanalysis, he moved away from experimental psychology, declaring twenty years later that, "whosoever wishes to know about the human mind will learn nothing, or almost nothing, from experimental psychology".

Family Life

Jung first saw Emma Rauschenbach (1882-1955) when she was sixteen, standing at the top of a staircase. He was twenty-one. Even before he spoke to her, he knew she would be his wife.

He said to a friend...

THAT GIRL IS MY WIFE!

Carl and Emma were married seven years later on 14 February 1903.

Emma came from an old Swiss German family and was an educated, handsome woman, well-liked for her charm and social grace. She was the daughter of a wealthy industrialist, and this gave Jung financial freedom to pursue his own work and interests.

The couple first lived in rooms at the Burghölzli, then, from 1909 onwards, in their newly built house on the lake at Kusnacht, near Zurich.

They had five children.

Agathe 28 December 1904

Gret 8 February 1906

Marianne 20 September 1910

Helene 18 March 1914

Franz 28 November 1908

From about 1911, Antonia Wolff became Jung's mistress, a relationship that lasted until her death in 1952. This triangular arrangement, difficult for both women, was tolerated by them and was known to the members of the Zurich analytic circle.

Emma and Antonia both worked with Jung and practised as analysts. Emma made a life-long study of Arthurian mythology. Her research on the Grail Legend was completed and published after her death by the Jungian analyst and scholar, Marie Louise von Franz.

Meeting Freud

Jung's work with the word association tests confirmed observations on the Unconscious already made by Freud. Jung sent him a copy of his results, and in 1906 the two men began a correspondence and friendship which lasted until 1913. Their initial rapport was immense and on Jung's visit to Freud in Vienna in 1907...

Jung's psychiatric background and experience at the Burghölzli, his intelligence and his growing repute, made him a valuable recruit to the psychoanalytic movement. And Jung had the advantage of not being a Jew.

GENTLEMEN WE NEED JUNG TO OVERCOME THE PREJUDICE THAT PSYCHOANALYSIS IS ONLY A JEWISH CONCERN!

Jung soon became a leading light in Freud's project. He was elected the first president of the International Psychoanalytic Association (IPA) and became the editor of its Jahrbuch, the first psychoanalytic journal.

How did it happen, then, that from being designated the "heir apparent of psychoanalysis" in 1909, only four years later he became for Freud...

...THAT BRUTAL AND SANCTIMONIOUS JUNG!

What were the reasons for the break?

(1) The Issue of Freud's Authority

In 1909, Freud and Jung travelled to the U.S. to lecture on psychoanalysis at Clark University. On the long sea journey, the two men analyzed each other's dreams, but Freud would not reveal the personal background details which interpretation required.

Freud was looking for a disciple who would accept his views without reservation, and he adopted a Father-stance with Jung.

JUNG WISHES TO KILL ME – THE FATHER OF PSYCHOANALYSIS – AND POSSESS PSYCHOANALYSIS, THE " BEAUTIFUL MOTHER", ALL FOR HIMSELF!

Freud had to resort to such "Freudian explanations" in order to deal with several uncanny incidents between the two men. Freud fainted twice in Jung's presence. On the first occasion, they were waiting to board ship for America. On the second, in 1912, they were having lunch at a conference in Munich following a long discussion about their divergences.

Psychoanalysis was threatening to split into tribal sects between Vienna (Freud) and Zurich (Jung), leaving Ferenczi to make the famous remark...

Sándor Ferenczi 1873-1933

... THE JUNG NO LONGER BELIEVE IN FREUD!

(2) Theoretical Differences

In his 1906 study on dementia praecox and association experiments, Jung acknowledged his indebtedness to the "brilliant discoveries of Freud".

He was also unenthusiastic about Freud's method of therapy.

Both men played down the importance of these disagreements, until their changing attitudes began to magnify them into unbridgeable gulfs.

The divergence emerged most publicly in Jung's lectures at Fordham University (New York) in 1912. Jung was supposed to be representing and defending psychoanalysis, but...

... HE'S CHALLENGING MY BASIC VIEWS AND REINTERPRETING EVERYTHING TO SUIT HIS OWN IDEA OF ANALYSIS!

Jung agreed with Freud that **hysteria** and **obsessional neurosis** show abnormal displacements of "quite definitely sexual libido", but...

... PSYCHOTIC STATES LIKE SCHIZOPHRENIA CANNOT BE EXPLAINED BY DISTURBANCES OF A SEXUAL NATURE.

This was because in cases of dementia praecox, individuals suffered a complete loss of reality.

I'M PLUM CAKE ON A CORNMEAL BOTTOM...

[AND SIGMUND DOESN'T UNDERSTAND A CASE LIKE MINE!]

"The loss of the reality function in psychosis is so extreme that it must involve the loss of **other** instinctual forces whose sexual character must be denied absolutely, for no one is likely to maintain that **reality** is a function of **sex**."

And what about Freud's theory of infantile sexuality?

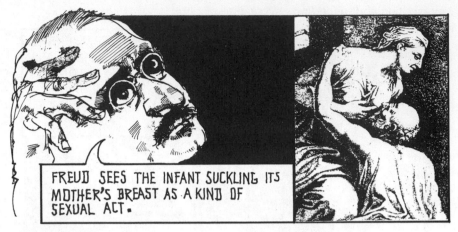

FREUD SEES THE INFANT SUCKLING ITS MOTHER'S BREAST AS A KIND OF SEXUAL ACT.

The emotional satisfaction of a child suckling is **only** the satisfaction anyone gets from eating.

To say it is evidence of an infantile sexual instinct confuses the adult **reproductive** instinct with a hunger drive common to all ages. Freud had over-extended the concept of sexuality in describing the development of psychic life from birth to maturity.

THERE'S NOTHING FOR IT BUT TO ABANDON THE SEXUAL DEFINITION OF PSYCHIC ENERGY.

AH, TRAITOR!

(3) Philosophical Differences

The split with Freud was deep-rooted in Jung's concerns about the mysterious nature of the soul.

FREUD ALSO HAS A MYSTICAL "NO. 2" SIDE, BUT ...

BAH, IT'S JUST REPRESSED SEXUALITY!

Although in this 1907-1913 period, Jung restricted his own Number 2 to the established limits of psychiatry and psychoanalysis, he maintained an active interest in parapsychology. In 1911, he began to study astrology.

DON'T WORRY! I'LL COME BACK FROM THE "RELIGIOUS LIBIDINAL CLOUDS" WITH A RICH BOOTY FOR ANALYSIS.

H'M... MAYBE WE CAN ANNEX PARAPSYCHOLOGY!

BUT REMEMBER – DON'T ABANDON THE SEXUAL THEORY! IT'S OUR ONLY DEFENCE AGAINST THE BLACK TIDAL MUD OF OCCULTISM...

AND THAT STRUCK AT THE HEART OF OUR FRIENDSHIP.

A Strange Incident

Jung was named "Crown Prince of the psychoanalytic movement" on the last night of his visit to Freud in March 1909. On that same evening, however, Freud's hostility to the occult irritated Jung, but he repressed an urge to reply sharply.

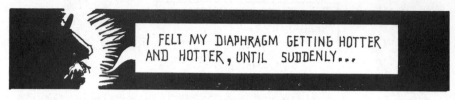

I FELT MY DIAPHRAGM GETTING HOTTER AND HOTTER, UNTIL SUDDENLY...

A loud noise came from the bookcase, as if it was going to topple on them.

THERE! THAT'S AN EXAMPLE OF A "CATALYTIC EXTERIORIZATION PHENOMENON".

OH COME — THAT'S SHEER BOSH!

IT'S NOT! AND TO PROVE MY POINT, I PREDICT **ANOTHER**

BANG

On the eve of his investiture as Crown Prince, Jung's Number 2 was stirring in an attempt to topple Freud's bookcase - the whole edifice of Freudian theory!

In 1909, Jung was immersed in studies of ancient mythology. Analyzing all those nymphs and centaurs ended up by confusing - and exciting - him.

> I FOUND MANY SIMILARITIES TO THESE MYTHS EXPRESSED BY THE INSANE.

For instance a Burghölzli patient...

> I SEE A PENIS COMING OUT OF THE CENTRE OF THE SUN, MOVING AND PRODUCING THE WIND

This made no sense, until Jung came across a reference to the pre-Christian Mithraic religion which described how the wind originated from a tube hanging from the centre of the sun.

> THE PATIENT KNEW NOTHING OF THIS MITHRAIC IMAGE - SO **WHERE** DID IT COME FROM?

Psychiatry recognized that the unconscious could retain "daily residues", images seen and forgotten and yet still stored in the subliminal mind, but Jung wondered if it could hold ancient or "archaic residues". Was the patient's image of the sun a collective, **inherited** image, harking back to forgotten mythologies buried in our unconscious?

The Case of Miss Frank Miller

Jung's interest was then drawn to an article written by a young American woman, Miss Frank Miller, which described a vision cloaked in unconscious "archaic residues".

WHAT I SAW AND HEARD IS TYPICAL OF A SEMI-CONSCIOUS OR "HYPNAGOGIC" STATE IN WHICH SPIRITUALIST MEDIUMS RECEIVE MESSAGES FROM THE DEAD...

...WHICH COME FROM SUBLIMINAL DAILY RESIDUES IN THE UNCONSCIOUS.

Miss Frank Miller

Théodore Flournoy 1854-1920 Experimental Psychologist

Jung had a different explanation.

MISS MILLER IS AN INTROVERT... HER PSYCHIC ENERGY HAS TURNED INWARDS TO PRODUCE THESE UNCONSCIOUS **ARCHAIC** RESIDUES...

THE FAILURE AND DEATH OF CHIWANTOPEL DRAMATIZES HER OWN FAILURE TO ACHIEVE THE HEROIC ACT OF SEPARATING FROM HER MOTHER...

... HER UNCONSCIOUS NEED TO SEPARATE AND HER INABILITY TO DO SO INDICATE THAT SHE TOO WILL BE "ENGULFED BY A LANDSLIDE".

Jung diagnosed a latent psychosis which would lead eventually to Miller's complete breakdown.

Jung published his analysis of Frank Miller, whom he had never met, regardless of her repute. In later editions, he added the information that his prognosis had "hit the mark in all essential respects" because Frank Miller had been admitted to a sanatorium, suffering from a schizophrenic collapse. The success of this prediction suggested that Jung's method could correctly diagnose psychological symptoms from **fantasies**, interpreted in line with mythological and historical images. This was proved true in subsequent cases, but Jung was wrong about Frank Miller. Recent research has shown that she **was** admitted to a sanatorium, but she had no hallucinations or delusions consistent with a schizophrenic condition, and she was discharged after a week.

Why did Jung get Frank Miller wrong? His struggle with Freud was moving to its crisis...

...BUT I WASN'T READY FOR IT.

AND YOU HAVEN'T SUCCESSFULLY CHALLENGED THE SEXUAL BASIS OF **NEUROTIC** DISORDERS THAT I HAVE DEMONSTRATED!

TO DEFEAT FREUD, I MUST SUPPLY A CONVINCING PROGNOSIS OF **PSYCHOTIC** DISORDERS...

In other words, if Jung's prediction of schizophrenia in Miller's case was proved right, he could force a wider definition of the psyche, beyond Freud's narrower theory of sexuality, and therefore redefine psychoanalysis.

45

Jung also disagreed with the basic "incest wish" that supported Freud's theory of the Oedipus Complex...

... THE CHILDHOOD FANTASY WISH TO MURDER THE FATHER AND POSSESS THE MOTHER.

FREUD TAKES THE INCEST WISH AS A **LITERAL** DESIRE TO PENETRATE THE MOTHER...

I SEE IT AS SYMBOLIC OF A DESIRE FOR SPIRITUAL **REBIRTH** IN THE PSYCHIC PROCESS OF BECOMING AN INDIVIDUAL.

But this idea of "archaic residues" in the unconscious was an expression of Jung's No.2 personality...

... THE BREATH OF THE GREAT WORLD OF STARS AND ENDLESS SPACE.

The Nekyia or Night-Sea Journey

After his split with Freud, Jung embarked on a perilous journey - the passage through mid-life crisis. Researches into mythology had acquainted Jung with age-old myths of the hero who must undergo a dangerous **Nekyia** or "night-sea journey". These heroic voyages are symbolized by the sun's own daily rising and falling, its "life" and "death"...

... AND ITS ANNUAL CYCLE THROUGH THE ZODIAC.

Sometimes the hero is devoured by a sea-monster...

... LIKE JONAH AND THE WHALE.

Or the monster is a devouring female...

... THE TERRIBLE MOTHER.

Psychologically, this is an unconscious image of our mothers to which we are attached and from which we must free ourselves in order to develop as separate, individuated beings. For this to happen the hero has to re-enter the mother (the belly of the whale) because only through such a re-entry can he be born again from her, this time spiritually. Such a re-entry has nothing to do with a sexual incest wish.

Jung had forecast his own unconscious voyage in Miller's case - and it was risky. He had seen the effects of the uncontrolled unconscious on the Burghölzli inmates, their minds flooded by an overwhelming sea of madness. Jung was in danger of a similar psychotic collapse.

Jung was 39 and he'd reached a dead-end. Friends and colleagues deserted him. He lost interest in scientific textbooks and he gave up his post at the university. Between 1914-1919, he withdrew from the world to explore his own unconscious.

I FELT LIKE THE HANGED MAN IN THE TAROT.

49

Alone on a Stone, Again

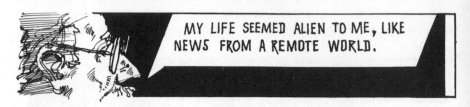

MY LIFE SEEMED ALIEN TO ME, LIKE NEWS FROM A REMOTE WORLD.

In the autumn of 1913, he had an overpowering vision.

"I saw a monstrous flood covering all the northern and low-lying lands between the North Sea and the Alps. When it came up to Switzerland I saw that the mountains grew higher and higher to protect our country. I realized that a frightful catastrophe was in progress. I saw the mighty yellow waves, the floating rubble of civilization, and the drowned bodies of uncounted thousands. Then the whole sea turned to blood."

The dream was repeated a few weeks later, accompanied by a voice which said "it is wholly real and it will be so". There followed a series of similar, ominous dreams which ended in June 1914 when he dreamed he came across a tree in a frozen landscape.

THE TREE WAS COVERED WITH SWEET GRAPES FULL OF HEALING JUICES THAT I PICKED AND GAVE TO A LARGE AUDIENCE.

When the Great War broke out in August 1914, he realized that the dreams were more than personal and he needed to understand "to what extent my own experience coincided with that of mankind in general".

Jung then decided to embark on a deliberate attempt to explore his own unconscious, allowing a stream of fantasies and images to arise as he played a childhood building game with stones at the shore of the lake. He "plunged down into dark depths", finding himself "at the edge of a cosmic abyss".

IT WAS LIKE A VOYAGE TO THE MOON OR A DESCENT INTO EMPTY SPACE. I FELT I WAS IN THE LAND OF THE DEAD!

Here he met and talked with the biblical characters of Elijah and Salomé, but the most important figure he encountered was called Philemon.

HE FLEW TO ME IN A DREAM – AN OLD MAN WITH BULL'S HORNS, HOLDING A BUNCH OF 4 KEYS, ONE READY TO OPEN A LOCK. HE HAD A KINGFISHER'S WINGS...

Jung did not understand the dream so he began to paint it and, as he did...

I FOUND A DEAD KINGFISHER BY THE LAKESHORE. I WAS THUNDERSTRUCK! KINGFISHERS ARE RARE IN OUR VICINITY AND I'VE NEVER SINCE FOUND A DEAD ONE.

This coincidence was one of the many he experienced throughout his life. It made the appearance of Philemon **real** for Jung. They went for walks up and down the garden and held philosophical discussions.

YOU'RE SAYING THAT MY THOUGHTS ARE NOT MY **OWN?**

OF COURSE THEY'RE NOT. YOU TREAT THOUGHTS AS IF YOU'D GENERATED THEM YOURSELF. BUT THOUGHTS ARE LIKE ANIMALS IN A FOREST OR PEOPLE IN A ROOM ... OR DO YOU THINK YOU'VE MADE **THEM** TOO?

Mythopoeic Imagination

Who or what is Philemon? From a psychiatric point of view, Jung was talking to himself and Philemon is a fantasy, a psychotic symptom, similar to the delusions and voices suffered by the schizophrenic.

YOU SPEAK TO HIM AS IF HE'S **REAL**.

YES, HE'S MY GHOST GURU SENT TO TEACH ME MY SPIRITUAL PATH.

Within the framework of Jung's later work in analytical psychology, Philemon can be labelled an "archetypal image of the spirit" from the fund of unconscious images which can fatally confuse the mental patient. But it is also the matrix of "mythopoeic imagination" which has vanished from our rational age. Though such imagination is present everywhere, it is both tabooed and dreaded.

The turning point was reached in the summer of 1916. Jung's house felt haunted, his daughters had seen ghosts and his son had dreamed of the devil fishing. It was a sunny afternoon, the main door of the house was open and the doorbell began to ring frantically.

SUDDENLY A WHOLE CROWD OF SPIRITS BURST INTO THE HOUSE!

WE HAVE COME BACK FROM JERUSALEM WHERE WE FOUND NOT WHAT WE SOUGHT.

Jung began writing, and as he did so, the whole ghostly assembly evaporated. For three days he was taken over by an episode of automatic writing, producing the **Septem Sermones** (The Seven Sermons).

Jung had come full circle from his student days when he had attended his cousin's séances. The medium now was not Helene Preiswerk, but Jung himself!

Mandala: the Path to the Centre

For the remainder of his life, Jung endeavoured to express the
insights which this exploration of the unconscious had brought. As
he moved towards the world again, Jung began to sketch small
circular drawings every morning which seemed to reflect his inner
state day by day.

THESE ARE EXACTLY LIKE **MANDALAS** USED IN EASTERN MEDITATION EXERCISES!

He saw that the mandala returned everything to a single central point
and interpreted this to mean that the goal of psychic development
was the "path to the centre, to individuation". The circular structure
of the mandala symbolized the **Self**, the totality of the individual,
conscious and unconscious, which carries an individual's sense of
meaning and purpose as he or she moves towards it.

This was confirmed to him in a dream years later in 1927. He dreamed of being in Liverpool - "the pool of life" - amidst rain, smoke and fog. On a small island in its centre, he came upon a beautiful magnolia tree in blossom.

I PAINTED THE DREAM, BUT WONDERED WHY IT FELT SO "CHINESE"...

Shortly afterwards, Richard Wilhelm sent him a manuscript of Chinese alchemical drawings, **The Secret of the Golden Flower**, requesting him to write a commentary on them.

CHINESE ALCHEMY LED ME TO SEE A COMMON PSYCHOLOGICAL BASIS UNDERLYING THE ANCIENT SYMBOL SYSTEMS OF DIFFERENT CULTURES.

Richard Wilhelm 1873-1930

Instincts and Archetypes

Jung had discovered that the delusions of the insane seemed to call on a **collective** fund of archaic images and symbols. His encounter with these images in his "nekyia" fully confirmed their existence. In 1919, Jung first used the term **archetype** in relation to such a memory. In addition to the personal unconscious, he posited a **collective unconscious** which is formed of two components, the **instincts** and the **archetypes**.

Instincts are impulses which carry out actions from necessity, and they have a biological quality, similar to the homing instinct in birds. **Instincts** determine our **actions**. Yet in the same manner, Jung suggests that there are innate, unconscious modes of understanding which regulate our **perception** itself. These are the **archetypes:** inborn forms of "intuition" which are the necessary determinants of all psychic processes.

As the instincts determine our actions, so the archetypes determine our mode of apprehension. Both instincts and archetypes are collective because they are concerned with universal, inherited contents beyond the personal and the individual and they correlate with each other.

How we apprehend a situation (archetype) determines our impulse to act. Unconscious apprehension through the archetype determines the form and direction of the instinct. On the other hand, our impulse to act (instinct) determines how we apprehend a situation (archetype).

Jung acknowledges this chicken-and-egg relationship and suggests that the archetype might suitably be described as the **instinct's perception of itself,** or as the "self-portrait of the instinct", in exactly the same way as consciousness is an inward perception of the objective life process.

Archetypes and Images

How are the archetypes known in our human experience? They have no material existence and reveal themselves only as **images**. For example, in all ages and cultures, mankind imagined itself in communion with a "Wise Spirit". One of the most common forms for this conception is the image of the Wise Old Man found in innumerable myths and legends.

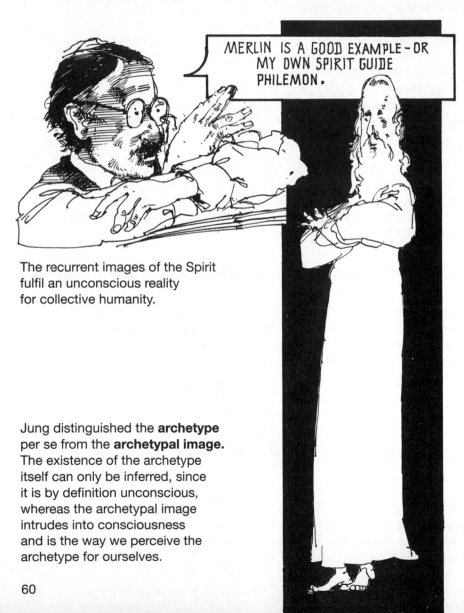

MERLIN IS A GOOD EXAMPLE – OR MY OWN SPIRIT GUIDE PHILEMON.

The recurrent images of the Spirit fulfil an unconscious reality for collective humanity.

Jung distinguished the **archetype** per se from the **archetypal image.** The existence of the archetype itself can only be inferred, since it is by definition unconscious, whereas the archetypal image intrudes into consciousness and is the way we perceive the archetype for ourselves.

Thus the archetypes, our modes of perception, both cloak and reveal themselves in images. Jung likens them to the axial system of a crystal's formation in the mother liquid. Archetypes are like **primordial ideas**, but are not abstract principles. They are **numinous**, electrically charged with a sense of the sacred.

ON SAFARI IN AFRICA IN 1925, I EXPERIENCED THIS NUMINOUS FEELING WITH EVERY DAWN SUNRISE...

Voyage into the Unconscious

Such an archetypal experience of sunrise is common to us all, throughout the history of all times and ages. The soul has a desire for light and an irrepressible urge to rise out of primal darkness. The moment in which light comes **is** God - it brings redemption, release.

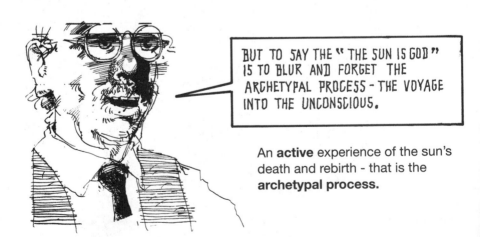

BUT TO SAY THE " THE SUN IS GOD " IS TO BLUR AND FORGET THE ARCHETYPAL PROCESS - THE VOYAGE INTO THE UNCONSCIOUS.

An **active** experience of the sun's death and rebirth - that is the **archetypal process.**

Some Basics of Jungian Analysis: (1) The Symbolic

How did Jung apply the archetypal process in analysis? A young, unmarried woman consulted him...

SHE ARRIVED TROUBLED BY FANTASIES, EXPRESSED IN SYMBOLS.

... A SNAKE COILED ROUND THE SUN, A PICKAXE AND A BURIED CROSS ...

BUT I HAVE NO IDEA WHAT THEY MEAN ...

DICTIONARY MEANINGS OF THESE SYMBOLS ARE EMPTY. YOUR EMOTIONAL RESPONSE IS WHAT MATTERS.

OF COURSE NOT, THEIR MEANING IS HIDDEN FROM YOUR CONSCIOUS CONTROL. SYMBOLS ARE CLUES, ACTIVATED BY YOUR OWN UNCONSCIOUS ENERGY.

The patient struggling to make sense of a disturbing symbol, an obscure dream or fantasy image, releases the unconscious meaning of the archetypes. Jung calls this the **transcendent function**, the archetypal process which brings into consciousness a previously unconscious content and restores the psyche to healthy balance.

(2) The Transcendent or Healing Function

For Jung, therapy must take a constructive and not reductive approach to the process of symbolic expression. Constructive treatment means paving the way for the patient's own insight into that process, often by seeking together for helpful parallels to the patient's own individual symbolism in ancient mythology.

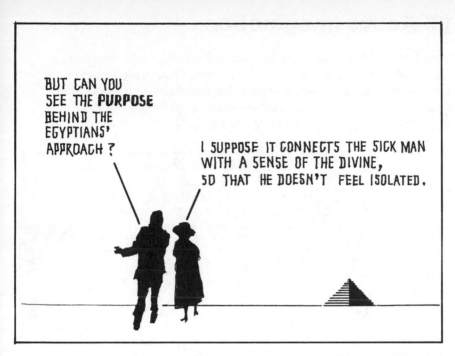

BUT CAN YOU SEE THE **PURPOSE** BEHIND THE EGYPTIANS' APPROACH?

I SUPPOSE IT CONNECTS THE SICK MAN WITH A SENSE OF THE DIVINE, SO THAT HE DOESN'T FEEL ISOLATED.

EXACTLY - HE FACES THE SAME DANGER AS A GOD - AND IT WAS HOPED THIS KNOWLEDGE WOULD HAVE A HEALING EFFECT.

Jung's own constructive practice was to reconnect the individual "with the gods" - that is, with the collective archetypes of the unconscious - so that the healing transcendent function could come into play.

65

(3) Active Imagination

Jung used many different approaches and techniques to reconnect his patients with the archetypes experienced through their images from dreams, fantasies and symbols. Psychoanalysis had employed hypnosis, automatic writing and free association to activate the unconscious mind...

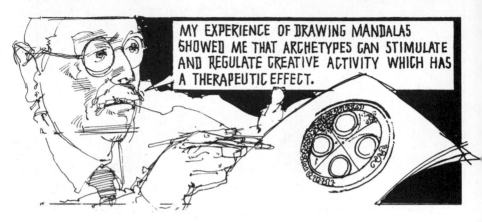

MY EXPERIENCE OF DRAWING MANDALAS SHOWED ME THAT ARCHETYPES CAN STIMULATE AND REGULATE CREATIVE ACTIVITY WHICH HAS A THERAPEUTIC EFFECT.

A dream image or symbol can be creatively elaborated in many ways...

... BY DRAMA, DANCE, PAINTING, WRITING...

... WHICH REDUCES THE INEXPLICABLE PRESSURE EXERTED BY THE UNCONSCIOUS AND ENCOURAGES THE PROCESS OF INDIVIDUATION.

Jung developed a method known as **active imagination**, a therapeutic process which climaxes in the patient's discovery of his or her own psychic centre.

(4) The Centring Process

The young woman reported a dream...

Unlike the process of active imagination, dream symbols are **passive**, emerging autonomously from the unconscious. The symbol "compensates" the dreamer for something lost or unknown - but what? Through the technique of **association**, the young woman has arrived at the personal context of her dream - a memory of her father. But more is needed.

Freud's analytical interpretation would reduce the sword immediately and obviously to a sexually compensating "father complex", a "penis envy fantasy". Jung's constructive approach instead employs the technique of **amplification** through which both the analyst and patient associate the sword with similar images found historically in myths and fairy-tales.

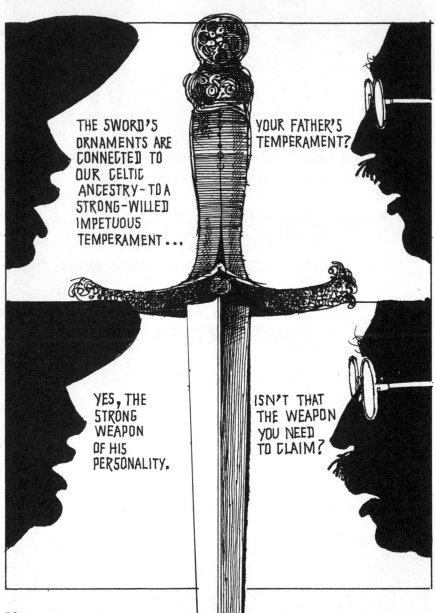

THE SWORD'S ORNAMENTS ARE CONNECTED TO OUR CELTIC ANCESTRY – TO A STRONG-WILLED IMPETUOUS TEMPERAMENT...

YOUR FATHER'S TEMPERAMENT?

YES, THE STRONG WEAPON OF HIS PERSONALITY.

ISN'T THAT THE WEAPON YOU NEED TO CLAIM?

The patient's own "weapon" has been brought to light through excavation - through constructive analysis - and she can now see that the sword, with its four-sided crucifix shape, is like the mandala, a symbol of her own **centre**.

UNTIL NOW, MY PERSONALITY HAS BEEN THAT OF A SPOILT CHILD, PASSIVE, COMPLETELY GIVEN TO SEXUAL FANTASIES.

THE FACT THAT I AM MY FATHER'S DAUGHTER HAS BEEN BURIED TOO LONG.

THE BURIED SWORD IS A NEGLECTED TRUTH ABOUT THE STRENGTH OF MY OWN PERSONALITY.

THE WILL BASED ON A KNOWLEDGE OF LIFE AND ON INSIGHT IS AN ANCIENT HERITAGE OF THE HUMAN RACE AND IT IS MINE TOO.

Dreams and Visions

Dreams, like visions, radiate from a hidden archetypal centre of meaning. Jung valued the prophetic meaning of both dreams and visions, such as Emanuel Swedenborg's telepathic vision of 1759.

Emanuel Swedenborg 1688-1772

On a Saturday in July 1759, Swedenborg was staying with friends in Gothenburg, 300 miles from Stockholm. At about 6 p.m. he went out alone, but returned pale and alarmed. "A fire has just broken out in Stockholm", he said, "and is spreading fast. A house of a friend is in ashes and my own is threatened." At 8 p.m. he exclaimed, "Thank God! the fire's extinguished, three doors from my house!"

On Monday and Tuesday, two different couriers arrived from Stockholm confirming in every detail Swedenborg's description of the fire. When asked how he'd known this, Swedenborg replied, "Angels told me."

Swedenborg's vision disobeys the normal laws of time and space, and plugs directly into the **collective** unconscious.

Jung believed that dreams, like various systems of divination, reveal **psychic** realities and sometimes offer a prophetic revelation.

Whatever emerges from the unconscious, whether it is an idea, image or an illusion, creates a **psychic reality**. It is a psychic condition of fact. Images from dreams or active imagination - or spirits like Philemon - are not simply delusions or fantasies.

WHAT IS AN ILLUSION?

DOES ANYTHING EXIST FOR THE PSYCHE THAT WE ARE ENTITLED TO CALL ILLUSION? THE PSYCHE DOESN'T TROUBLE ITSELF ABOUT OUR CATEGORIES OF REALITY. FOR IT EVERYTHING THAT **WORKS** IS REAL.

On this "workable" basis, Jung developed his analytical psychology to explore the nature of psychic reality.

Building Stones...

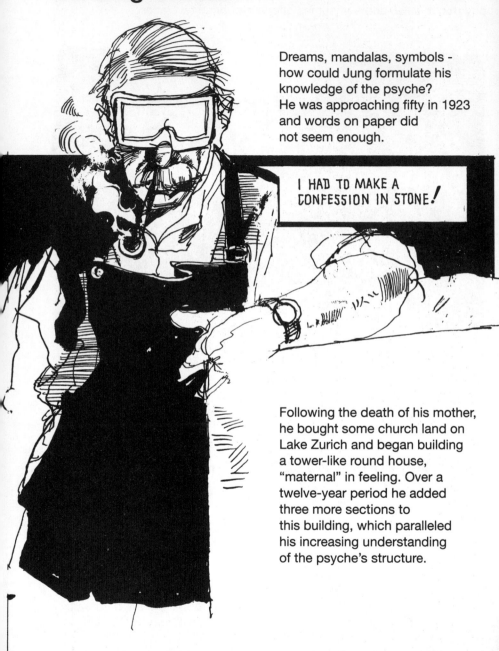

Dreams, mandalas, symbols - how could Jung formulate his knowledge of the psyche? He was approaching fifty in 1923 and words on paper did not seem enough.

I HAD TO MAKE A CONFESSION IN STONE!

Following the death of his mother, he bought some church land on Lake Zurich and began building a tower-like round house, "maternal" in feeling. Over a twelve-year period he added three more sections to this building, which paralleled his increasing understanding of the psyche's structure.

...the Bollingen House

Bollingen, with its silence of the dead, became Jung's spiritual retreat. With no electricity or running water, it put him in touch with nature and his "No. 2" the "age-old son of the mother".

The original building was low and crouching, reflecting his own introversion, but after his wife's death in 1955 when he was eighty, he felt confident enough to add a second storey. This represented an "extension of consciousness achieved in old age", a feeling of being reborn in stone as he completed his own self-development and moved towards death.

Jung's Practice of Analytical Psychology

Jung named his method **Analytical Psychology** to distinguish it from psychoanalysis. A large clientele gathered round him and many went on to train as analysts themselves. Jung warned his students against becoming dependent on any one method.

3 DO'S...

1 Analysis is face-to-face participation and each case is unique. **"Remember, only the wounded physician heals."**

2 In surgery and obstetrics it is accepted that the doctor must have clean hands. **"So make sure you're 'clean' of neuroses yourself."**

3 Jung was the first psychoanalyst to advocate a **training** analysis for therapists - and further ongoing supervision, some sort of "mother or father confessor". **"Even the Pope has a confessor."**

The purpose of therapy is **progressive** and not **regressive**, which means focusing on the conscious attitude of the patient's current position.

1 Don't go chasing after infantile memories.

> NEUROTICS LIKE NOTHING BETTER THAN WALLOWING IN THE EVILS OF THE PAST AND SELF-PITY.

2 Don't forget spiritual issues.

> MOST WHO ENTER ANALYSIS AFTER THEIR MID-LIFE CRISIS DO SO BECAUSE OF NEGLECTED SPIRITUAL ISSUES DURING THE FIRST HALF OF LIFE.

3 Don't forget the patient's personal **secret** story.

> THE PATIENT HAS A STORY THAT ISN'T TOLD AND WHICH NO ONE KNOWS OF. IT IS THE SECRET, THE ROCK AGAINST WHICH HE IS SHATTERED.

The Structure of the Psyche

Jung's analytical psychology involves a "structure" and a dynamic of the psyche. By **psyche**, Jung means the whole of our being, conscious and unconscious. It is innately purposeful or **"teleological"**, seeking growth, wholeness and equilibrium. It is distinguishable from his concept of the **Self**, which stands for the goal towards which the psyche is oriented.

The psyche is divided into consciousness and the unconscious and the latter serves to **compensate** the conscious attitude. Whenever the conscious attitude is too one-sided, its unconscious opposite manifests itself **autonomously** (Greek: **auto**=self, **nomos**=law, a law unto itself) to rectify the imbalance. It does this internally through powerful dreams and images, or it can pathologize in disease.

Frequently an unconscious component can externalize and appear from without, and is known as **projection**. This involves an excessive emotional response to another person or situation, like falling in love or disliking someone intensely. Such powerful emotional responses may indicate that an unconscious content is seeking to burst through into consciousness, but it can only appear as externalized, or projected onto the other person. It is not the other person we love or hate, but part of ourselves projected onto him or her.

Locating the direction of psychic energy is a key part of the analyst's task, and as an aid to such analysis Jung developed a series of **psychological types**.

Psychological Types: (1) Two Attitudes

Jung divided psychic energy into two basic attitudes - **extrovert** and **introvert** - which are present in everyone to varying degrees.

Extrovert

An extrovert attitude is motivated from the outside and is directed by external, objective factors and relationships.

PSYCHIC ENERGY FLOWS OUTWARDS TOWARDS THE WORLD.

Introvert

An introvert attitude is motivated from within and directed by inner, subjective factors.

WITHDRAWING ENERGY FROM THE WORLD.

You can see these attitudes in Freud and Jung's conflict of philosophies. Extroverts and introverts tend to misunderstand and disrespect each other.

Extroversion and introversion are mutually exclusive. If one forms the habitual conscious attitude, the other becomes unconscious and acts in a compensatory manner.

If the conscious attitude becomes too fixed, its unconscious attitude will break through as "the return of the repressed".

Jung's classification has become so influential that the terms "extrovert" and "introvert" are now part of everyday speech. We commonly use them to describe recognizable forms of social behaviour.

(2) Four Functions

Besides these two attitudes, Jung introduced four functional types - a four-part structure or **quaternity** which resembles the mandala.

NATURE HAS 4 SEASONS AND 4 COMPASS POINTS...

And ancient Greek medicine identified 4 types of human temperaments or "humours".

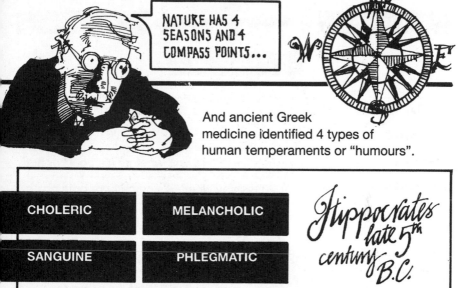

CHOLERIC	MELANCHOLIC	*Hippocrates late 5th century B.C.*
SANGUINE	PHLEGMATIC	

BASED ON 4 QUALITIES

HOT	COLD
DRY	MOIST

AND 4 ELEMENTS

FIRE	EARTH	*Empedocles mid 5th century B.C.*
AIR	WATER	

Jung recognized that "quaternities" could be used to describe the character of the psyche.

Jung posits **four functions** of the psyche, grouped into two pairs of opposites.

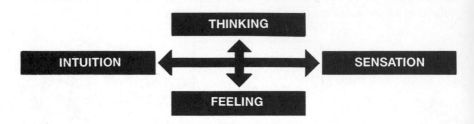

THINKING	
INTUITION	SENSATION
FEELING	

SENSATION	Tells you something exists
THINKING	Tells you what it is
FEELING	Tells you whether it's good or not
INTUITION	Tells you where it's come from or is going

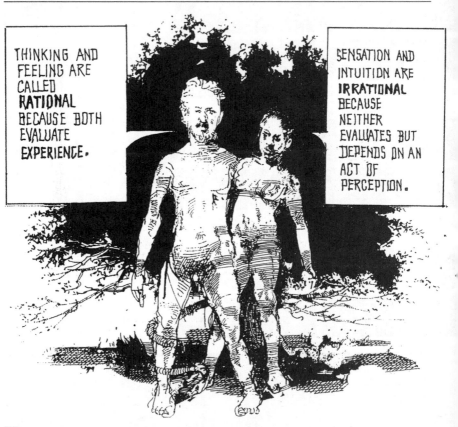

THINKING AND FEELING ARE CALLED **RATIONAL** BECAUSE BOTH EVALUATE EXPERIENCE.

SENSATION AND INTUITION ARE **IRRATIONAL** BECAUSE NEITHER EVALUATES BUT DEPENDS ON AN ACT OF PERCEPTION.

An individual's innate conscious orientation will be towards one of these four.

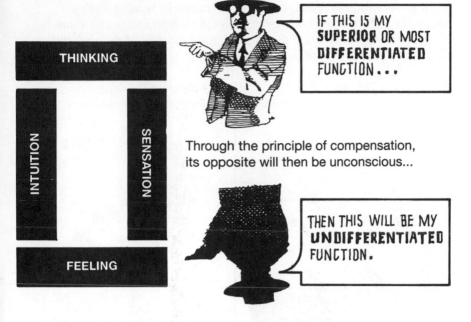

THINKING

INTUITION

SENSATION

FEELING

IF THIS IS MY **SUPERIOR** OR MOST **DIFFERENTIATED** FUNCTION...

Through the principle of compensation, its opposite will then be unconscious...

THEN THIS WILL BE MY **UNDIFFERENTIATED** FUNCTION.

The leftover other two, as partially conscious or **auxiliary** functions, may serve the superior function.

The Return of the Repressed

The over-developed thinking type may be subject to unbalanced moods and upsets.
A feeling-type boy could be forced to develop thinking characteristics by a thinking-type father, creating crisis and unhappiness in later life.
Repressed feeling returns as hysteria. Repressed sensation manifests in phobias, compulsions and obsessions.
Mental and physical health therefore depend on

A the development of the neglected function -

B awareness of the 4 types at work in oneself to achieve a rounded personality.

Eight Psychological Types

Jung combined the **two attitudes** with the **four functions** and created **eight psychological types**. Locating the person's type enables the analyst to make better sense of an individual's world-view and value system. The types describe personality and frequently determine the choice of vocation or marriage partner.

1. Extrovert Thinking
Examples: scientists, economists

2. Introvert Thinking
Examples: philosophers

WE DISCOVER NATURAL LAWS...

Charles Darwin

...AND CREATE THEORETICAL FORMULATIONS

Karl Marx

WHAT IS THINKING?

Ludwig Wittgenstein

They direct themselves and others according to fixed rules and principles. They are "interested" in reality, order and material facts.

They formulate questions and seek to understand their own being. They neglect the world and dwell on their own ideas.

3. Extrovert Feeling
   Examples: chat show hosts, stars

Conventional and well-adjusted to their time and milieu, they are concerned with personal and social success. They are changeable and into fashions.

WE BEGIN AND END RELATIONSHIPS QUICKLY.

Frank Sinatra

WE CAN BE MOODY, SENTIMENTAL, SURPRISING.

Madonna

4. Introvert Feeling
   Examples: monks, nuns, musicians

They are inaccessible, but appear harmonious and self-sufficient. They can be involved in poetry and music. "Still waters run deep" is the impression they give.

WE'RE MYSTERIOUS AND ENIGMATIC...

Chopin

... AND YOU ATTRACT POWERFUL EXTROVERT MEMBERS OF THE OPPOSITE SEX!

5. Extrovert Sensation
   Examples: builders, speculators

They focus on external facts, are practical, hard-headed and accept the world as it is. Affable enjoyers of life, but their sensuality can breed addictions, perversions and compulsions.

WE SEEK PLEASURE THROUGH THE 5 SENSES!

Casanova

6. Introvert Sensation
Examples: connoisseurs, aesthetes

They feed on sense impressions and immerse themselves in their own inner sensations.
They are aesthetic, often unassuming and bemused.

WE CAN HAVE DIFFICULTY IN EXPRESSING OUR OWN VISION AND CREATIVITY.

The Aesthete

7. Extrovert Intuition
Examples: PR people, adventurers

Unconscious insight keeps them on the scent of future novelty. Trouble-shooters, often charismatic leaders, but their ruthless adventuring makes them unfit for long-term stability.

OUR PROJECTS OR RELATIONSHIPS TEND TO GO HAYWIRE!

Robert Maxwell

8. Introvert Intuition
Examples: mystics, poets

They follow an inner vision, day-dreamers, often gifted in clairvoyance, seeing themselves as misunderstood geniuses struggling with a unique, esoteric experience.

WE CAN SEEM LIKE CRANKS TO OTHERS.

William Blake

Different types frequently intermarry, each unconsciously relying on the other to take care of his or her inferior function.

Contrasting types may put each other down and complementary unions are not the solution to individual psychic wholeness.

Same-type marriages can double up on the superior function and increase the disruptive power of the inferior function.

Jung was aware that typologies do not express the unique complexities of any one person. People are a mixture of types which needs lengthy observation and analysis. An individual can also change types at different stages of life. But types are useful in describing how the individual will respond to **archetypal figures**.

Four Archetypal Figures

The psychological types are part of a broader dynamics of psychic energy which involves **4 Archetypal Figures.** These figures work together in **pairs**, one of which is conscious and compensated by its unconscious counterpart.

Pair 1: Ego and Shadow

Jung remembered a dream from his student days. On a dark night of fog and high wind...

I STRUGGLED TO PROTECT MY LIGHT FROM THE WIND...

A GIGANTIC BLACK SHADOW BEGAN FOLLOWING ME...

MY OWN SHADOW CAST 'BY MY LIGHT!

The light and shadow were Jung's own Number 1 and Number 2 personalities, which he later identified as the related archetypal figures, the **Ego** and the **Shadow**.

THE EGO IS THE FRAGILE, PRECIOUS LIGHT OF CONSCIOUSNESS THAT MUST BE GUARDED AND CULTIVATED.

One of the first steps in analysis is to make the patient aware of the "Ego-Shadow" relationship. The shadow is always of the **same** sex.

THE EGO IS YOUR SENSE OF PURPOSE AND IDENTITY.

A healthy Ego organizes and **balances** the conscious and unconscious elements of the psyche. A weakened Ego leaves an individual "in the dark", in danger of being swamped by chaotic unconscious images.

AND THE SHADOW? IT IS OUR OWN " DARK SIDE", CHARACTERIZED BY INFERIOR, UNCIVILIZED OR ANIMAL QUALITIES WHICH THE EGO WISHES TO HIDE FROM OTHERS.

NOT WHOLLY BAD, BUT PRIMITIVE AND UNADAPTED. IT CAN VITALIZE LIFE, IF WE HONESTLY FACE UP TO IT.

Ego and Shadow are personified by Dr. Jekyll and Mr.Hyde, the classic "good and bad" split in all of us. Mr. Hyde becomes a real danger to psychic health when the Ego itself screws up. How can this happen?

Although the Ego is the centre of consciousness, it should not be confused with the **Self** which is the final goal of the individuation process, the **wholeness** of the personality.

THE EGO WHICH IDENTIFIES WITH THE SELF BECOMES INFLATED, DANGEROUSLY GOD-LIKE.

An inflated Ego projects its own irrational Shadow onto others and identifies **them** as evil.

The mass psychosis of Hitler's Nazi Germany and its genocidal atrocities occurred because the German Ego became inflated through its identification with the "pure Aryan race" and projected its **Collective Shadow** onto the Jews.

The individual patient in the early stages of Jungian analysis who "encounters the Shadow" faces a crisis. The more he recognizes and withdraws from the Shadow projections, the more he feels his Ego threatened.

THE LESS I CAN SAY - "**THEY** DO THIS, **THEY** ARE WRONG, **THEY** MUST BE FOUGHT " - THE MORE I BECOME A SERIOUS PROBLEM TO **MYSELF!**

YOU'RE BEGINNING TO REALIZE THAT WHATEVER IS WRONG IN THE WORLD IS IN **YOURSELF.** LEARN TO DEAL WITH YOUR **OWN** SHADOW AND YOU'LL DO SOMETHING REAL FOR THE WORLD.

Collective Shadow

The psyche is not confined to individuals only, but has a collective nature too, structured in the same way as the individual. The collective psyche forms the "Zeitgeist" or spirit of the age.

One example of the collective psyche's Shadow is Nazi Germany. But it can be seen in any mass movement, trend or gathering. A crowd at a football match forms a collective ego which casts a Shadow - uncontrolled hooliganism.

The collective Shadow can also be cast by a scientific event. When the first atom bomb mushroomed in the desert dawn of Alamagordo, Oppenheimer called it...

J. Robert Oppenheimer
1904-1967

... BRIGHTER THAN A THOUSAND SUNS!

Atomic physicists in the USA had won the race against Nazi Germany to "split the atom". But this scientific achievement, "brighter than a thousands suns", means we now live with the darkest shadow humanity has ever known.

Pair 2: The Persona and the Soul-Image

The Ego is related to what Jung calls the **Persona**, that part of consciousness which "negotiates" with the outer world on the Ego's behalf. Persona comes from the Latin word for "theatre mask".

IT'S THE FACE WE WEAR FOR SOCIETY.

The Persona is conditioned by social class, job, culture and nationality. There are often several personas we use to suit different situations. But we adopt a general Persona based on our **superior** functional type (e.g. thinking) because it comes easiest to us.

Psychic health and equilibrium depend on a well-adapted Persona because it makes social exchange possible.

The "perfect Persona" can lead to a one-sided, rigid and alienated personality.

Neurosis can arise from "wrong answers to life", from empty success and confinement within too narrow a spiritual horizon. Neurosis generally disappears by developing into a more spacious personality.

Male and Female Soul-Images

The unconscious side of the Persona is the Soul-image. Jung uses the Latin male and female names for the soul, the **animus** and the **anima**. The Soul-Image is always represented by the individual's opposite gender.

A MAN'S
SOUL-IMAGE
IS FEMALE:
THE **ANIMA.**

THE WOMAN'S
SOUL-IMAGE IS
MALE: THE
ANIMUS.

The Soul-Image is an archetype which can represent the whole of the unconscious. It is inherited, collective and "ageless".

BUT IT IS MODIFIED
BY ONE'S ACTUAL
EXPERIENCE OF THE
OPPOSITE SEX,
ESPECIALLY
OF PARENTS.

Soul-Images appear in dreams, myths and fantasies, but they are also **projected**.

GIVING A DISTORTED IMPRESSION
OF INDIVIDUALS OF THE OPPOSITE SEX.

The Anima

The male's Soul-Image has appeared in many forms throughout the ages, but always with the compelling and fascinating secret nature of **Eros** (love), as an archetype of life itself, represented in images of earth and water.

Identifying completely with the anima can lead to effeminate homosexuality or transvestism.

The Animus

The woman's Soul-Image takes the nature of **Logos** (reason), the search for knowledge, truth and meaningful activity, often represented by images of air and fire.

The animus is projected onto men with whom she is emotionally involved.

FATHER FIGURES IN A YOUNG WOMAN.

HEROIC MEN AS SHE MATURES.

COMFORTING MALE FIGURES LIKE DOCTORS OR PRIESTS AS SHE GROWS OLD.

Over-identification with the Soul-Image produces the **Sol Niger** or Black Sun, the animus-dominated woman - obstinate, ruthless and domineering, craving power and irrationally opinionated.

SOL NIGER IS PREJUDICED AND AS UNTEACHABLE AS A BLIND TOM CAT.

Complementary Images

Jung believed men were polygamous in their conscious attitude, and so the anima compensates as only **one** woman in the unconscious.

Because women are monogamous in their conscious attitude, the animus appears in compensatory form as a **group** of men.

SHE CAN ALSO APPEAR AS A CAVE, SHIP, BOWL, PURSE, CAT, COW ETC.

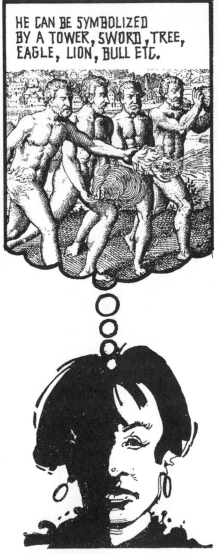

HE CAN BE SYMBOLIZED BY A TOWER, SWORD, TREE, EAGLE, LION, BULL ETC.

Mixed Types

The pairing of conscious Persona and unconscious Soul-Image is coloured by the **2 attitudes** and the **4 functions**. The conscious Persona is based on the dominant attitude. (e.g. extrovert) and **superior** function (e.g. feeling). Hence the unconscious Soul-Image counterpart will be imagined along lines of the opposite attitude and inferior function.

So, besides an extrovert/introvert "switch", the following happens:

thinking persona	=	feeling soul-image
intuitive persona	=	sensation soul-image
feeling persona	=	thinking soul-image
sensation persona	=	intuitive soul-image

A thinking-type man, cut off from the realm of feeling, may dream of mermaids or he may project his unconscious, undifferentiated feeling-function onto a feeling-type woman with whom he falls in love. By embracing her, he indirectly embraces his own feeling nature. But as he becomes more aware of his unconscious feeling through the relationship, the anima image holds less fascination for him. His projection will be withdrawn and he falls out of love. As we go through life it becomes less easy to fall in love in a romantic way because in the process of self-development we gradually integrate more and more of our unconscious contents.

Jung's Women

Jung discovered the anima during his night-sea journey when he heard a woman's voice trying to seduce him into the erroneous belief that...

> THE FANTASIES YOU'RE WRITING DOWN ARE **ART.**

> ARGUING WITH HER MADE ME REALIZE SHE WAS A NEGATIVE ASPECT OF MY ANIMA, FULL OF DEEP CUNNING.

By believing his experiences were only "art", Jung might have been able to dismiss them easily, without feeling any moral obligation towards them. The negative form of the anima, either in dreams or when projected onto a woman, can be disastrous for a man.

> THE INSINUATIONS OF THE ANIMA, THE MOUTHPIECE OF THE UNCONSCIOUS, CAN UTTERLY DESTROY A MAN!

After the negative "Frank Miller" episode, most of Jung's encounters with the anima were positive. Many of his followers were women, partly due to his sexual charisma, but also because they were in therapy with him.

BECAUSE I EXPLORE WHAT WESTERN CULTURE CALLS "FEMININE CONSCIOUSNESS"...

HE BECOMES AN ANIMUS FIGURE FOR WOMEN, ATTRACTED LIKE BEES TO A HONEY POT!

Jung's wife Emma had to contend with this "animus harem" and at least one mistress. She confided to Freud, back in 1911....

NATURALLY ALL THE WOMEN ARE IN LOVE WITH HIM. CARL SAYS I SHOULD STOP CONCENTRATING ON HIM AND THE CHILDREN, BUT WHAT ON EARTH AM I TO DO?

Emma eventually became an analyst herself and made a life-long study of the Grail legend.

Women played key roles in the advancement of Jung's career. In February 1916, soon after Jung's split with Freud, the Analytical Psychology Club was founded in Zurich - and from the start women were active participants in it.

This is also true of the C.G. Jung Institute, founded in 1948, which continues to teach and practice today.

A third important platform for disseminating Jung's work was the Eranos Conference. It was initiated in 1923 by Olga Frobe-Kapteyn, a Swiss, at her villa at Lake Maggiore, Italy, and became the annual "happening" of analytical psychology and its links with Eastern philosophy.

Edith Rockefeller McCormick
American. Analyzed by Jung between 1913-1923. Became a patroness and financed the meeting place for the Analytical Psychology Club in Zurich in 1916.

Sabina Speilrein
Russian Jew. Began an analysis with Jung in 1904 which developed into an intimate but stormy relationship. Later trained with both Jung and Freud and became an analyst. Returned to Russia where she and her children became victims of the Germans during the Second World War.

Antonia Wolff (1888-1953)
Swiss. Began analysis with Jung in 1910 and soon became his mistress, a relationship which lasted until her death. She assisted him in his work and trained and practised as an analyst, publishing in the Jungian journals.

Esther Harding

(1888-1971)Met Jung in England and followed him to Zurich for analysis and training. Moved to the US and founded the Analytical Psychology Club in New York and later the Institute. Published **Women's Mysteries** and **The Way of All Women**.

Mary Mellon

(1904-1946) American.
In analysis with Jung, inspired by his ideas and attended his seminars. Founder of the Bollingen Foundation which published the Eranos lectures and Jung's collected works.

Olga Frobe-Kapteyn

Analyzed by Jung and developed work on active imagination and links with Eastern thought. Collaborated with Mary Mellon to publish the Eranos papers and Jung's collected works.

Aniela Jaffe

German. Analyzed by Jung and trained and practised as an analyst. Secretary of the Institute (1955-1961) and Jung's private secretary working with him to produce his autobiography.

Jolanda Jacobi

(1890-1973) Hungarian. Trained with Jung and practised as an analyst, publishing several books on his methods. She was a key mover in the founding of the Institute.

Marie-Louise Von Franz

(born 1915) German. Met Jung when she was eighteen and became his assistant after graduating in linguistics. She translated Latin texts and collaborated on his alchemical studies. Analyzed and trained by Jung, she has been involved with Analytical Psychology all of her adult life and has remained a leading light of the Institute in Zurich.

A Stone in Space

Early in 1944, in his 69th year, Jung fell and broke his foot. Following this, he had a heart attack. In a drugged state and close to death, he fell into an unconscious delirium and had an **out-of-body** experience.

I SAW A TREMENDOUS DARK BLOCK OF STONE IN SPACE LIKE A METEORITE. I HAD SEEN STONES LIKE THAT IN THE GULF OF BENGAL HOLLOWED OUT INTO TEMPLES. AN ENTRANCE LED INTO A SMALL ANTECHAMBER I ENTERED AND SAW A HINDU...

I'VE BEEN EXPECTING YOU.

It was time for Jung to "enter his stone".

HERE I WOULD AT LAST UNDERSTAND WHAT HAD BEEN BEFORE ME, WHY I HAD COME INTO BEING, AND WHERE MY LIFE WAS FLOWING!

At that moment, a face floated up from earth - a Greek king or **basileus** from the island of Kos on which the temple of the healing god Asklepios was sited.

AHA! THIS IS MY DOCTOR. BUT HE'S COME IN HIS PRIMAL FORM, AS BASILEUS OF KOS...

YOU'RE NOT GOING TO DIE, NOT YET.

As soon as the doctor told him he must return, the vision ceased.

"4.4.44"

Jung was disappointed and resented coming back to life. He was also worried that the doctor had appeared in his "primal form", because it meant a fatal exchange had been made.

THIS MEANS DR H WILL HAVE TO DIE IN MY PLACE...

HIS LIFE'S IN DANGER – BUT HE WON'T LISTEN TO ME!

WHY DO YOU KEEP CALLING HIM "BASILEUS OF KOS"? IT'S SO UNFRIENDLY.

DON'T WORRY HE'S JUST HALLUCINATING.

Doctor

When Jung was allowed to sit up for the first time, he was struck by the date 4th April 1944.

ON THIS DAY – 4.4.44. – DR H TOOK TO HIS BED AND DID NOT LEAVE IT AGAIN. HE DIED SOON AFTERWARDS OF SEPTICAEMIA.

As he slowly recovered, Jung had further visions, and night after night he lived in a state of bliss. These experiences were utterly real, with a quality of objective truth.

WE SHY AWAY FROM THE WORD "ETERNAL", BUT I REALLY EXPERIENCED THE ECSTASY OF A NON-TEMPORAL STATE IN WHICH PRESENT, PAST AND FUTURE ARE ONE.

After this illness and near-death experience, Jung's principal works were written. During his seventies, that strange "something" called the soul was proving stronger than ever, and Jung was now prepared to give it voice.

The Uncanny

As we have seen, Jung was no stranger to the uncanny. He had seen ghosts in his own house and had once been driven out of a house in England by a female ghost that terrified him.

On his way home one day...

> IMAGES OF SOMEONE DROWNING KEPT FLASHING INTO MY MIND.

> ON MY ARRIVAL, I DISCOVERED THAT MY YOUNG GRANDSON'S BOAT HAD CAPSIZED IN THE LAKE AND HE'D NEARLY DROWNED.

On another occasion, at a wedding reception , he struck up a conversation with a man about criminal psychology.

> TO ILLUSTRATE MY IDEAS, I MADE UP AN IMAGINARY BUT DETAILED CASE HISTORY.

> AN EMBARRASSING SILENCE DESCENDED ON THE TABLE.

Afterwards, Jung was taken aside and scolded. The story he had made up fitted perfectly the life history of the stranger he was talking to!

As an analyst and doctor, Jung always watched for "omens" which might arise around his patients. For example, a patient's wife told Jung that...

AT THE DEATH OF MY GRANDMOTHER AND MOTHER, BIRDS GATHERED OUTSIDE THEIR WINDOWS.

This story alerted Jung to some apparently innocuous symptoms in his patient.

HMM! YOUR THERAPY IS NEARLY OVER, BUT SOMETHING WORRIES ME. I THINK YOU SHOULD SEE A HEART SPECIALIST.

The man went, but the specialist found nothing wrong with him. On his way back, Jung's patient collapsed in the street and was brought home dying. His wife was already in panic, because soon after her husband had gone to the doctor...

A WHOLE FLOCK OF BIRDS SETTLED ON THE HOUSE!

WHEN A TRANSFERENCE OCCURS ON THE PATIENT'S PART - A MORE OR LESS UNCONSCIOUS BOND WITH THE DOCTOR - THIS CAN SOMETIMES LEAD TO PARANORMAL EVENTS. I'VE OFTEN RUN INTO THIS.

Jung's intuitive gifts, coupled with the sheer force of his personality, led to his being seen as a guru figure, the "wise old man" of Kusnacht. His acceptance of the psychic reality of omens led naturally to the exploration of divination - especially the Chinese oracle book, the **I Ching** or **Book of Changes.**

Since 1920, Jung had been fascinated with the **I Ching**. One summer in Bollingen, he cut himself a bunch of oracle reeds.

I SAT FOR HOURS BENEATH A 100-YEAR-OLD PEAR TREE, PRACTISING THE I CHING TECHNIQUE. ALL SORTS OF UNDENIABLY REMARKABLE RESULTS EMERGED.

What is the link between **psychic** and **physical** events?

Jung used the **I Ching** with his patients. For example, a young man with a strong mother complex felt unsure about marrying a certain girl.

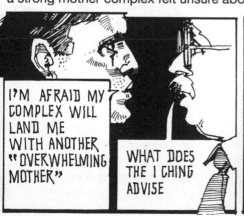

I'M AFRAID MY COMPLEX WILL LAND ME WITH ANOTHER "OVERWHELMING MOTHER"

WHAT DOES THE I CHING ADVISE

" THE MAIDEN IS POWERFUL. ONE SHOULD NOT MARRY SUCH A MAIDEN".

I CHING

歸妹

Jung was acutely aware of the "pernicious misunderstandings" which exist among Westerners hostile to divination. Advising an unknown correspondent not to establish an I Ching Institute, Jung warned him...

TO AVOID THE DISASTROUS PREJUDICE OF THE WESTERN MIND, YOU WILL HAVE TO INTRODUCE THE MATTER UNDER THE CLOAK OF SCIENCE.

Once again, we see the ambiguous relationship between Jung's Number 2 world of the mystic diviner, and the Number 1 area of the scientist and rationalist. This contrast is persistent throughout Jung's life and work. It is the antagonism of opposites - mind and matter, spirit and body, order and chaos, eternity and death, etc. - which underlies all of Western thought itself.

Psychology of Religion

As a scientist and rationalist - what was Jung looking for in the "psychology of religion"?

What we call "religion" evolved through a series of stages...

Archaic Stage

shamans, medicine men and sages

Ancient Civilizations

prophets, physicians and priests

The Christian Heritage

mystics, theologians and philosophers

All these religious figures, at every stage of history, share one thing in common - the inner experience of divinity. Jung calls this experience, **numinous** (from the Latin, **numen** or **numina**, "the presiding god".)

When the shaman hears...

THE VOICE OF THE GREAT SPIRIT.

Or the Christian mystic experiences...

THE CHRIST WITHIN.

Both are referring to an archetype of **wholeness**, the archetype of **Self**, represented as an image of God.

All religions confirm the existence of "something whole", independent of the individual ego and whose nature transcends consciousness.

What the numinous experience of "inner divinity" really points to is the process of **individuation**.

The archetype of wholeness manifests itself in dreams, myths and fantasies. It occupies a central position in the unconscious and tends to relate all other archetypes to this centre which is approximate to the God-image.

Symbolism of the Catholic Mass

When the Christian faith speaks of "salvation through Christ", it is referring to the individuation process (salvation) and an image of wholeness or Self (the God-image, Christ). This individuation process is ritually dramatized by the Catholic mass in which the bread and wine symbolize Christ.

Rituals in which a god is transformed into food and eaten existed long before Christianity. Jung mentions an Aztec rite. A dough was made out of the seeds of the prickly poppy...

IT WAS MOULDED INTO THE FIGURE OF THE GOD HUITZILOPOCHTLI.

This god figure was dismembered, distributed and eaten by the worshippers.

The eating of Christ's "body and blood" in the Catholic mass not only commemorates his sacrifice and death, but symbolizes his resurrection and **transmutation** into the immortal body of his Church.

Sacrificial dismemberment, death and rebirth are ritual steps of a transmutation process also undergone by tribal shamans from archaic times even to this day.

The shaman's spirit "leaves his body" and goes on a visionary pilgrimage, during which he experiences...

Sickness

Torture

Death

and Rebirth

What a shaman experiences is similar to Christ's passion, but also parallels the soul's after-life voyage towards rebirth in Tibetan Buddhism, the Egyptian **Book of the Dead** and many other religions.

In other words, these spiritual experiences of death and rebirth communicate a process of becoming **whole** through sacrifice.

YOU ARE CHANGED IN SUBSTANCE... OR TRANSUBSTANTIATED... TRANSFORMED, EXALTED, LITERALLY "SELF-ENHANCED".

The drama of the Catholic mass arose from the same psychic processes underlying other ancient pagan rituals.

Christ, an Archetype of the Self

Jesus is known as "the Christ", from the Greek **Khristos**, meaning anointed King or Messiah. But he has many other titles.

SON OF MAN. THE SECOND ADAM. SHEPHERD AND SACRIFICIAL LAMB OF GOD. FISH AND FISHER OF MEN.

FROM A PSYCHOLOGICAL POINT OF VIEW, CHIRST IS THE **ORIGINAL MAN**.

He represents wholeness of personality which surpasses and includes the ordinary man.

Jung defines the "whole person" as the **Self**. In the archetypal symbolism of the Mass, Christ represents the Self, and the Mass itself dramatizes the individuation process. The mystery of the Eucharist transforms the soul of the empirical man, who is only a part of himself, into his totality, symbolically expressed by Christ.

In early mystical Christianity, Christ had represented a totality that even embraced the anima or **Shadow** side of man. But the Church later developed an extremely one-sided image of Christ.

HE WAS CONCEIVED "IMMACULATELY"

A redeemer - all goodness and light - who reflects a perfectly good Father...

··· A GOD OPPOSING THE DEVIL AND THE DARK FORCES OF EVIL.

AND I'M EXCLUDED!

The Christ symbol lost its wholeness, in a psychological sense, by creating an opponent Shadow.

The Faust Legend

Goethe's **Faust** tells the story of a 16th century German alchemist who sold his soul to Satan in exchange for diabolical powers. Faust is profoundly significant because he exemplifies the spiritual dilemma of modern scientific man.

HE FORMULATES A PROBLEM THAT HAS BEEN BREWING FOR CENTURIES...

... HOW TO FREE OURSELVES FROM THE OPPOSITES OF GOOD AND EVIL, SPIRIT AND MATTER, FAITH AND KNOWLEDGE, ETC.

Faust dreams of possessing Helen of Troy.

HIS SOUL-IMAGE OR ANIMA WITH WHOM HE MISTAKENLY IDENTIFIES. AND I, MEPHISTOPHELES, AM FAUST'S OWN SHADOW.

The Faust drama exemplifies the difficulties of individuation for persons in the Christian and scientific worlds.

Jung saw much of himself in Faust, inspired in part by a family rumour that suggested he might be Goethe's illegitimate great grandson.

Johann Wolfgang Von Goethe 1749-1832

The Fourth Term

Western man's Faustian struggle with the dark side of human nature is rooted in a theological problem. How can an omnipotent, all-good God allow the existence of evil? If God did not create the Devil, then the latter must be self-creating, implying that God is not omnipotent. Evil must therefore be created by man's choice, by his Original Sin which Christ's sacrifice was meant to redeem.

Such an irreducible divide between good and evil means that Christianity cannot unite the opposites found in nature. Most religions address the problem of opposites - good and evil, male and female, yin and yang, etc. But Christianity equates the feminine either with an immaculate Virgin Mary or with the wicked temptress Eve.

The sexual nature of the feminine is darkened and repressed, leaving a Christ-figure so over-identified with light that he inevitably casts a Shadow. An early sect of heretic Christian mystics, the Gnostics, had tried to complete the Trinity of Father, Son and Holy Ghost with a **fourth term** - the darker, mysterious, feminine dimension of nature.

In 1950, the Pope declared the doctrine of the Blessed Virgin's Assumption - her literal "heavenly transportation" and reunion with the Son as the Celestial Bride. Jung saw this as the Church's unconscious recognition of the "fourth term". He called it "the most important religious event since the Reformation".

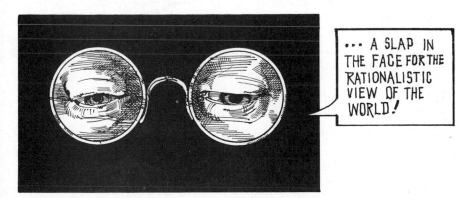

... A SLAP IN THE FACE FOR THE RATIONALISTIC VIEW OF THE WORLD!

"We must be deliberately blinding ourselves if we cannot see its symbolic nature and interpret it in symbolic terms".

The Age of the Fishes

You are looking
at an image of the fixed stars
that make up the constellation of
Pisces. The constellation is pictured as two
fishes (Latin, **pisces**) joined to each other by a "cord" of
stars. The fish on the left appears to swim vertically and the one
on the right horizontally to the **ecliptic**. What is the ecliptic?

The earth goes round the sun in one year. But from our viewpoint on
earth, it seems as if the sun is going round the earth against a
background of constellations.

This yearly "great circle" which the sun appears to trace in a sky of fixed
stars is known as the **ecliptic**.

Every year around 21 March, the sun crosses the equator, making day
and night of equal length. This is called the Spring Equinox
(equinox=equal night). The place on the ecliptic where the sun appears
at this moment is called the **Spring Equinox Point**.

At the annual Spring Equinox, the sun comes back to the same position on the ecliptic. Well, almost but not quite! The Spring Equinox Point slips back along the ecliptic by a small amount every year. In 72 years, the Spring Point is 1 whole degree further back along the ecliptic. This backwards movement is known as the **Precession of the Equinoxes**.

Jung used the constellation of these "paired fishes" to interpret the problem of **opposites** in Christianity, inextricably knotted together as the "fish of spirit" (on the left) and the "fish of matter" (right). He demonstrates this conflict by studying the precession of the equinoxes along the ecliptic. This is Jung's grandest and most ambitious interpretation. How does he proceed?

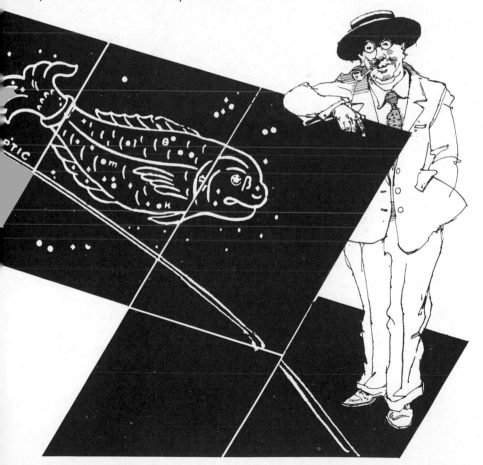

The Birth of Christ in Pisces 1

Let's look more closely at Pisces 1. Jung shows that Christ's birth occurs when the Spring Point is aligned with the star called Al Rischa or the "Knot" where the cord linking the two fishes, and first fish itself, begins.

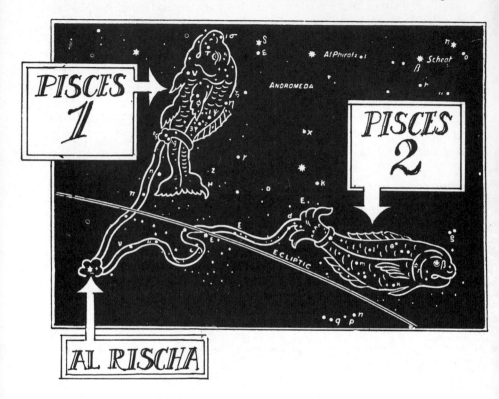

At about this time, in 7 B.C., the star of Bethlehem appeared, which wasn't a star at all but an unusual triple conjunction of the planets Jupiter and Saturn. This triple sighting of the "Star" became personified by the Three Wise Men for whom it heralds the coming of the King (Jupiter) of the Jews (Saturn). Christ is symbolized by Pisces 1, the "fish of spirit", a messiah who announces the new Age of Pisces.

It is astonishing that the star of Bethlehem should appear "by coincidence" at the Spring Point of Pisces, at the inauguration of the New Age. But it is also intriguing that in this age, the "fish" was used as a name and symbol for Christ, the God "who became a man".

BORN AS A FISH WHO HAD FISHERMEN FOR DISCIPLES.

I HAVE COME TO MAKE FISHERS OF MEN.

WHO FED THE MULTITUDE WITH MIRACULOUSLY MULTIPLYING FISH.

WHO WAS HIMSELF EATEN AS A FISH THE "HOLIER FOOD".

WHOSE FOLLOWERS WERE KNOWN AS LITTLE FISHES, THE **PISICULI.**

There is no evidence that the fish symbolism was being consciously employed.

IT JUST SEEMS TO HAVE HAPPENED NATURALLY, WITHOUT ANYBODY THINKING ABOUT IT.

The Spread of Christianity

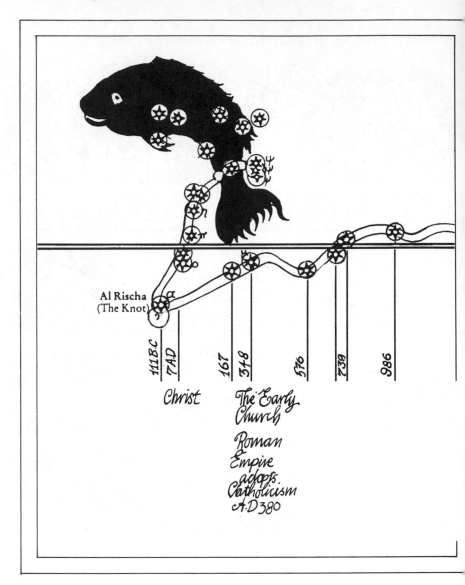

As the Spring Point moves along the ecliptic in alignment with the stars in Pisces 1, the Christian church grows, strengthens and develops its image of the unblemished, all-good Christ, the King or all-powerful Pantokrator.

Moving towards the Antichrist

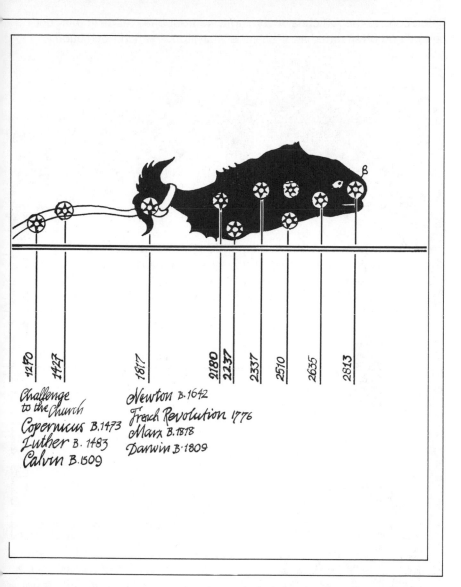

1270
1427
1817
2180
2237
2337
2510
2655
2813

Challenge to the Church
Copernicus B.1473
Luther B. 1483
Calvin B.1509

Newton B.1642
French Revolution 1776
Marx B.1818
Darwin B.1809

But then, as the Spring Point passes along the cord uniting the two fishes, heretical doctrines begin to flourish, culminating in the Reformation and violent religious conflicts throughout Christendom. Christianity itself was disintegrating as Europe underwent the Renaissance era of voyages, discovery, science and neo-paganism.

Prophecies of the Antichrist

Predictions of the Antichrist's coming were frequently made in this "cord" period, and often dated as 1789 - the year of the French Revolution.

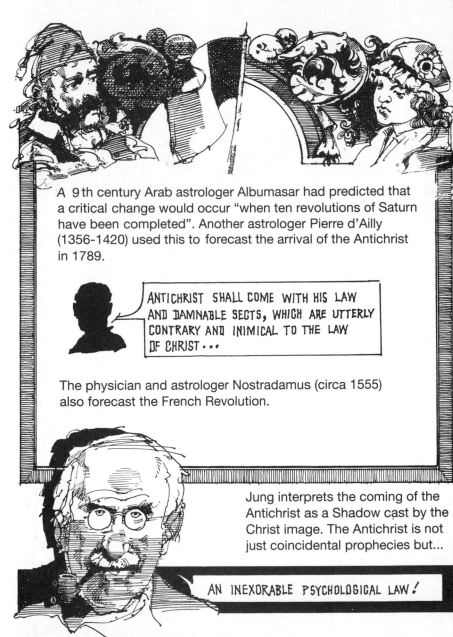

A 9th century Arab astrologer Albumasar had predicted that a critical change would occur "when ten revolutions of Saturn have been completed". Another astrologer Pierre d'Ailly (1356-1420) used this to forecast the arrival of the Antichrist in 1789.

ANTICHRIST SHALL COME WITH HIS LAW AND DAMNABLE SECTS, WHICH ARE UTTERLY CONTRARY AND INIMICAL TO THE LAW OF CHRIST ...

The physician and astrologer Nostradamus (circa 1555) also forecast the French Revolution.

Jung interprets the coming of the Antichrist as a Shadow cast by the Christ image. The Antichrist is not just coincidental prophecies but...

AN INEXORABLE PSYCHOLOGICAL LAW!

The Mirror-Image Opposite

The Spring Point reached the first star in the tail of Pisces 2 in 1818. We now come to the enantiodromian or "mirror-image opposite" of Christianity, to an era of generally **anti**-Christian ways of thinking.

The "birth of the Antichrist" occurs with the French Revolution, when a statue to the Goddess of Reason was enthroned in the cathedral of Notre Dame in Paris. Anti-Christian **materialism** would soon be established by Charles Darwin (born 1809) and Karl Marx (born 1818).

Charles Darwin 1809-1882

Karl Marx 1818-1883

Scientific Rationalism

Western thinking in the 19th and 20th centuries has eliminated what Jung calls the "mythopoeic imagination".

The bridge of spiritual experience which once crossed the divide of opposites has collapsed, because it failed the empirical "cause and effect" test of science.

Jung's work in the last part of his life focussed on giving both worlds of science and mythopoeic imagination their due. His old Number 1 and Number 2 personalities were now located in the whole project of Western civilization.

The Psychology of Alchemy

Jung found the historical equivalent to his own psychology in medieval **alchemy** (from the Arab, **al** "the", and Greek **khemia,** "art of transmuting metals"). Alchemy had discovered its own peculiar solution to the problem of uniting the opposites.

COLLECTED A LIBRARY OF ALCHEMICAL MANUSCRIPTS AND BEGAN TO DECIPHER THEM.

He was the first to make alchemy **psychologically** accessible to the 20th century by showing how alchemical symbols were similar to archetypal dream images.

The Alchemist's Stone

Alchemy is called the "hermetic art", a secret or occult practice named after the legendary founder of alchemy, Hermes Trismegistus, the "thrice-greatest Hermes". What was the alchemist's goal?

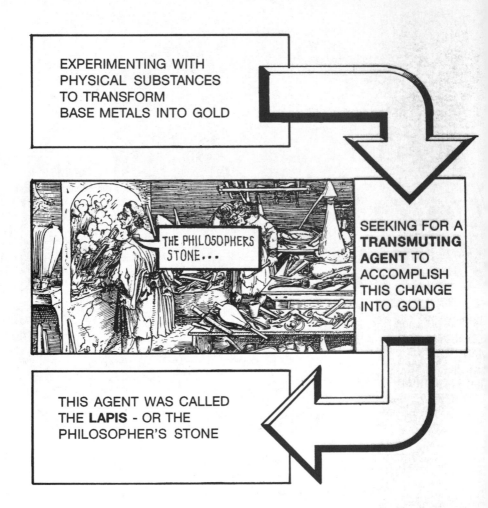

EXPERIMENTING WITH PHYSICAL SUBSTANCES TO TRANSFORM BASE METALS INTO GOLD

THE PHILOSOPHERS STONE...

SEEKING FOR A **TRANSMUTING AGENT** TO ACCOMPLISH THIS CHANGE INTO GOLD

THIS AGENT WAS CALLED THE **LAPIS** - OR THE PHILOSOPHER'S STONE

It is likely that the alchemist's aim was not to produce real material gold but "philosophic" gold. They were concerned not only with the transformation of inanimate matter but with their own **spiritual** transformation.

Jung believed that alchemy stood as the Shadow in compensatory relationship to Christianity. Christianity's one-sided dogma and inability to unite the opposites had alienated us from our natural roots in the unconscious.

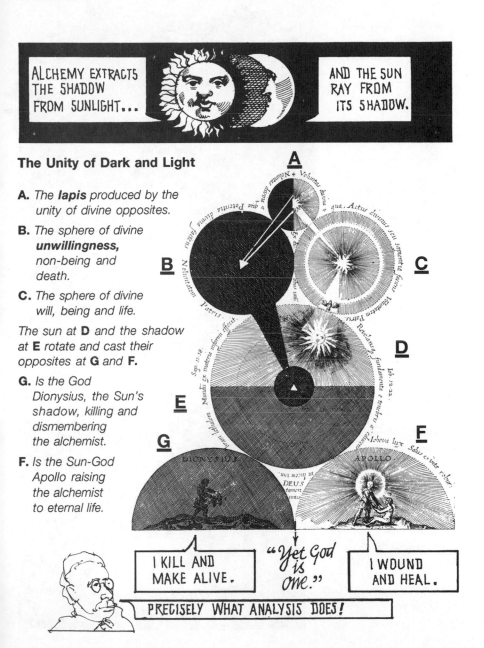

ALCHEMY EXTRACTS THE SHADOW FROM SUNLIGHT...

AND THE SUN RAY FROM ITS SHADOW.

The Unity of Dark and Light

A. The **lapis** produced by the unity of divine opposites.

B. The sphere of divine **unwillingness,** non-being and death.

C. The sphere of divine will, being and life.

The sun at **D** and the shadow at **E** rotate and cast their opposites at **G** and **F.**

G. Is the God Dionysius, the Sun's shadow, killing and dismembering the alchemist.

F. Is the Sun-God Apollo raising the alchemist to eternal life.

I KILL AND MAKE ALIVE.

"Yet God is one."

I WOUND AND HEAL.

PRECISELY WHAT ANALYSIS DOES!

Jung suggests that alchemists became increasingly aware of the mystical nature of their work. The **Lapis** became identified not only with the alchemist himself...

...BUT WITH CHRIST!

In the Christ=Lapis= alchemist equation they saw their goal not only as assisting God to redeem man, but also to redeem God himself from matter. The one primarily in need of redemption was not man, but the deity sleeping in the darkness of matter!

Jung had found **his** stone again in the **Lapis** - the Philosopher's Stone - which was a symbol of the Self. He agreed with the instruction of the 16th century master alchemist, Gerhard Dorn, who said, "Transform yourselves into living Philosophical Stones!"

Jung recognized that the alchemical work parallels the individuation process. The analytical task is identical to the alchemical endeavour.

WHY IS
THAT?

BECAUSE BOTH THE ANALYSAND AND ALCHEMIST ARE "PATIENTS" WHO MUST UNDERGO AN INNER JOURNEY.

Both are "patients" (from the Latin root, **pati**, "suffer") because both must confront the terrors of their own unconscious in a process that aims at total transformation. Both are projecting their unconscious into the "darkness of matter" in order to illuminate and liberate it - or to bring it to consciousness.

The alchemist is often depicted as working with a female assistant, the anima or soul-image. The materials they "cook" and "brew" can be paired with psychological equivalents. For instance, sulphur is "hot and desirous".

SILVER IS RETENTIVE AND TOUCHY.

IRON IS BRAVE AND PASSIONATE.

COPPER IS CONSTANT AND SENSUOUS.

HONEST, LOFTY TIN.

AND DETACHED, CRUEL LEAD.

The Spirit of Mercurius

The slippery nature of mercury with its invisible, poisonous vapours epitomized the dangers, tricks and deceptions of the entire work. The Spirit of Mercurius is the central figure through whom the alchemical union of opposites is made possible. Mercurius is for Jung the image of the **collective unconscious** itself.

"I am the old dragon, found everywhere on the globe of the earth, young and old, very strong and very weak, death and resurrection, visible and invisible, hard and soft; I descend into the earth and ascend into the heavens, I am the highest and the lowest, the lightest and the heaviest...I am dark and light...I am known and yet do not exist at all."

Stages in the Individuation Process

Alchemists experimenting in their laboratories reported confrontations with terrifying monsters in their retorts and alembics. Jung recognized those monsters as archetypal images which describe the psychic conditions of the alchemist undergoing states of depression, despair, passion, frustrated desire and so on. These could be paralleled to the stages in the individuation process during analysis.

REBUILDING THE PERSONALITY FROM START TO FINISH IN ANALYSIS.

The Chemical Marriage

Throughout the alchemists' recipes for making the stone, Jung found a constant theme of a "chemical marriage" between a King and Queen (gold and silver) who unite, die and are reborn as a Siamese-paired **hermaphrodite**. Jung studied the bizarre imagery of this marriage with immense difficulty in 1955 when he was 80 and his own wife died.

THE MARRIAGE OF KING AND QUEEN DESCRIBES ANALYSIS ITSELF, ESPECIALLY THE **TRANSFERENCE** RELATIONSHIP BETWEEN ANALYST AND PATIENT.

Jung interpreted some woodcut illustrations from a 17th century alchemical text, the **Rosarium Philosophorum**, to describe the process of analysis in archetypal terms.

LET'S SEE HOW THIS LOOKS.

The Rosarium Philosophorum - or - Philosophers' Rose Garden

1. The Mercurial Fountain

The vessel in which the work takes place contains the divine water. The stars at the four corners are the 4 elements in separate and hostile states which need to be united, as the 5th star over the fountain shows. These four elements are Jung's **four functions**, and the 5th is the wholeness of Self.

The stars on the vessel represent six planets, and the triple fountain in its middle is the seventh, Mercury. The Mercurial Fountain is a "chthonic" or underground counterpart to the Christian Trinity.

MERCURY'S WATER CAN CAUSE GREAT ELATION AND DEPRESSION ...

... JUST AS I'LL EXPERIENCE IN THERAPY.

Mercurius is also the water in the fountain and symbolizes the unconscious. The process begins with disunion, a disintegrated and unredeemed state among the four elements or functions. Redemption or wholeness will be effected through Mercurius, the integration of unconscious elements.

2. King and Queen

The King and Queen are the Sun and Moon, animus and anima, brother and sister. They are fully clothed, disguising their natural state. Their left-handed handshake indicates a **sinister** union. The left is the dark unconscious side which suggests an incestuous marriage. In their right hands, the King and Queen hold branches with 4 flowers, the 4 elements. The dove, or Holy Ghost, descends and unites them in a union which is also spiritual. Incest, the union of like with like, symbolizes marriage with one's being, becoming the Self, individuation.

OUR CROSSED BRANCHES SHOW OUR RELATIONSHIP STARTS AT "CROSS PURPOSES",...

THE RELATIONSHIP COMBINING ALL POSSIBLE CONSCIOUS AND UNCONSCIOUS STAGES.

The King and Queen are the **unconscious** figures of the alchemist and his female anima assistant.

In terms of the **transference**, this is the initial meeting of the analyst and patient.

The "incestuous" handshake indicates that unconscious infantile fantasies, originally invested in members of the patient's family, are transferred onto the analyst and provide the "primal matter" for the analytical work.

3. The Naked Truth

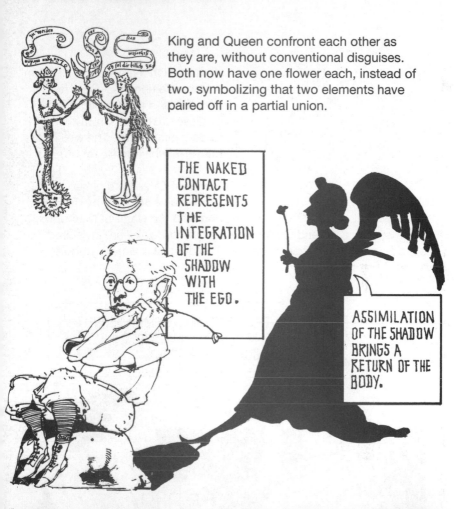

King and Queen confront each other as they are, without conventional disguises. Both now have one flower each, instead of two, symbolizing that two elements have paired off in a partial union.

THE NAKED CONTACT REPRESENTS THE INTEGRATION OF THE SHADOW WITH THE EGO.

ASSIMILATION OF THE SHADOW BRINGS A RETURN OF THE BODY.

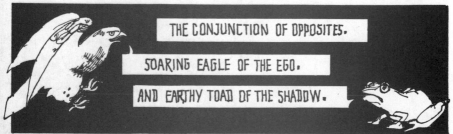

THE CONJUNCTION OF OPPOSITES.

SOARING EAGLE OF THE EGO.

AND EARTHY TOAD OF THE SHADOW.

Animal instinct and primitive consciousness merge without being repressed by fictions or illusions.

4. Immersion in the Bath

King and Queen descend into the water - the unconscious. The immersion is a night-sea journey or dissolution which returns them to dark initial state. The well is a uterus in which to be reborn.

King and Queen are united "above and below" - by the dove and also the water of Mercurius, the unconscious. King and Queen - or Spirit and Body - are unrelated without the soul to bind them together. The dove and water symbolize the bond of the soul.

THE UNRELATED HUMAN BEING CAN ACHIEVE WHOLENESS ONLY THROUGH THE SOUL...

5. The Coniunctio or Intercourse

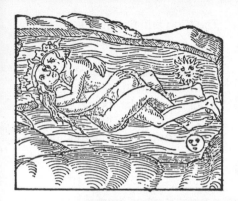

The sea now engulfs the King and Queen. Their coitus occurs in water, in the unconscious. They have returned to the beginning - the **massa confusa** or "unleashed chaos" - and at this moment the **Lapis** is conceived.

6. Death and Putrefaction

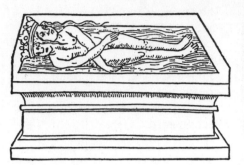

The King and Queen are dead and have melted into a being with two heads, the **hermaphrodite**. After intercourse, a state of putrefaction sets in, a punishment for the sin of incest and conception. This is known as the **nigredo** state of blackness which requires the alchemist's self-cleansing.

The nigredo indicates that psychic life stagnates when there is a blending of identity into the unconscious. It also represents the stage in analysis when projections are withdrawn.

THIS ENLARGES THE PERSONALITY, BUT CAN ALSO LEAD TO EGO INFLATION...

... IF THE EGO IDENTIFIES WITH UNCONSCIOUS CONTENTS AND IS THEREBY "POLLUTED" BY THEM.

When the Ego unites successfully with the unconscious soul-image, it will produce a new personality compounded of both, the self or union of opposites.

7. Ascent of the Soul

The Soul departs from the Spirit and Body of King and Queen in great distress. Unlike the usual idea of conception, it does not come from "above" to animate the body, but it leaves the body to mount heavenwards. Later, it will descend as a healing force and saviour, a parallel to Christ's Second Coming.

The alchemist putrefying in the inside of the philosopher's egg - a stage of suicidal depression.

This is the soul-less stage in analysis when the patient has no sense of direction, as in schizophrenia. The decomposition of the elements, the 4 Functions, has led to dissociation and collapse of the existing ego consciousness. The analyst, like the alchemist, must work ceaselessly at this stage to assist the royal couple's "resurrection".

8. Purification

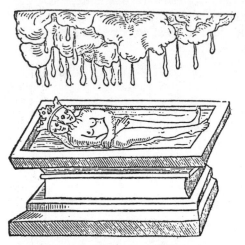

The dew descends - the **aqua sapientiae** or Water of Wisdom - portending the divine birth. Illumination washes away the nigredo by an **albedo** or whitening, like sunrise after darkness.

At this stage of analysis, when the unconscious contents have been made conscious and theoretically evaluated, the patient usually believes the goal has been reached.

149

9. The Return of the Soul

The Soul dives from heaven to breathe life into the hermaphrodite. Yet two ravens at the bottom of the picture indicate that a pair of opposites still exists in the sphere of the unconscious. The winged and wingless birds symbolize the double nature of Mercurius, the **chthonic** (earthy underworld) and **pneumatic** (airy, upperworld) sides.

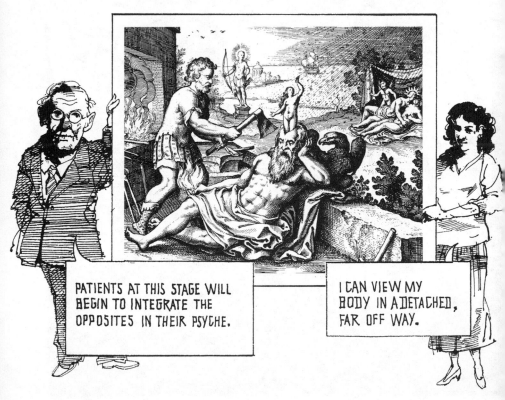

PATIENTS AT THIS STAGE WILL BEGIN TO INTEGRATE THE OPPOSITES IN THEIR PSYCHE.

I CAN VIEW MY BODY IN A DETACHED, FAR OFF WAY.

10. The New Birth or Rebis

The **Rebis**, or the "reborn" is winged hermaphrodite standing on the Moon, with snakes and a raven still present - creatures associated with the Devil. Why is the desired goal of alchemy portrayed in this monstrous form?

BECAUSE ALCHEMY IS THE "MATERNAL DARKNESS" THAT COMPENSATES FOR CHRISTIANITY'S "PATERNAL LIGHT".

AND THE GOAL IS TO BECOME WHOLLY ONESELF! LIGHT AND DARK MADE ONE.

The importance of Jung's alchemical studies extends far beyond their relevance to analytical psychology and into the mystery of the "mind-matter" connection itself. Located prior to modern physics, alchemy crossed the divide between psyche (spirit) and matter, subject and object. As chemistry and physics developed out of alchemy into objective sciences, the psyche of the observer became specifically excluded from the objective material with which the observing scientist worked. It was therefore only in the twilight paranormal area that the mysterious union of psyche and matter could be emotionally experienced in our modern age. The alchemists had named this union the **Unus Mundus**, "One World". It was this experience of "oneness" that Jung attempted to elucidate through his concept of **synchronicity**.

Synchronicity

"Meaningful coincidences" had always fascinated Jung. He looked for a theoretical concept that would account for such paranormal "chance" phenomena as the I Ching. In 1930, he first used the term **synchronicity** to describe an "**a-causal** connection between psychic states and objective events." Here is an example of synchronicity from a patient's case history.

At that moment, Jung heard a gentle tapping at the closed window behind him. He turned and saw a flying insect knocking at the glass.

Jung opened the window and caught the insect as it flew in.

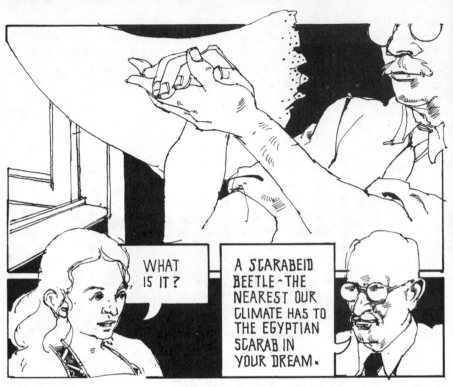

WHAT IS IT?

A SCARABEID BEETLE - THE NEAREST OUR CLIMATE HAS TO THE EGYPTIAN SCARAB IN YOUR DREAM.

The patient had no idea that the golden scarab was an Egyptian symbol of rebirth. But the "coincidence" of that common rose-chafer beetle flying in through the window suddenly gave her dream a new significance. It helped her break free of her over-logical animus shell.

NOW MY SPIRITUAL REBIRTH CAN BEGIN!

Most spontaneous "synchronistic" events like this one usually had a direct psychic connection with an archetype.

Is it "meaningful" or is it just coincidence?

Jung carefully distinguishes synchronicity from the mere "synchronism" of events occurring simultaneously but unconnected in meaning. Everyday life often provides us with a common type of synchronicity.

There are more eerie precognitive and clairvoyant synchronicities, such as Swedenborg's vision.

Commenting on Swedenborg's state of mind, Jung says that a lowering of the threshold of consciousness must have given him access to "absolute knowledge". The fire in Stockholm was, in a sense, burning in him too. For the unconscious, space and time seem relative - knowledge finds itself in a space-time continuum in which space is no longer space, nor time time.

Qualitative Time

Jung's early attempts to understand synchronicity were influenced by a classical idea of astrology, the "objective time moment". This supposes that certain **quality** exists in a moment of time itself - "a time to be born, a time to die, a time to reap and a time to sow". Whatever is done at **this** moment of time, has the quality of **this** moment of time.

Qualitative time seems to "explain" why astrology and other forms of divination work.

But synchronicities are not always dependent on such a moment of time. Precognition, for instance, does not occur in "same-timeness". Jung gradually abandoned the supposition of qualitative time. He concluded that since qualitative time is nothing but the flux of things, and is just as much "nothing" as space, this hypothesis ends up in a vicious circle - "the flux of things and events is the cause of the flux of things, etc."

Sir James Jeans 1877-1946

Synchronicity and Post-Einsteinian Physics

Jung went on wondering if there was any **law** or pattern of synchronistic events which could be contrasted with the physical law of causality. He thought it possible to link his "a-causal principle" of synchronicity to new ideas now emerging in physics - which also suggested an a-causal paradox.

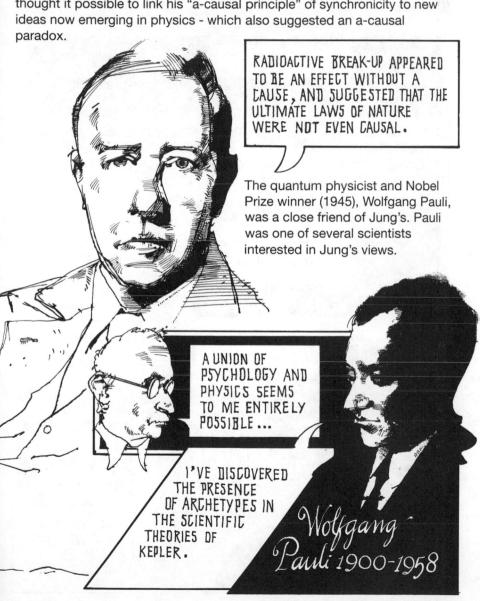

RADIOACTIVE BREAK-UP APPEARED TO BE AN EFFECT WITHOUT A CAUSE, AND SUGGESTED THAT THE ULTIMATE LAWS OF NATURE WERE NOT EVEN CAUSAL.

The quantum physicist and Nobel Prize winner (1945), Wolfgang Pauli, was a close friend of Jung's. Pauli was one of several scientists interested in Jung's views.

A UNION OF PSYCHOLOGY AND PHYSICS SEEMS TO ME ENTIRELY POSSIBLE ...

I'VE DISCOVERED THE PRESENCE OF ARCHETYPES IN THE SCIENTIFIC THEORIES OF KEPLER.

Wolfgang Pauli 1900-1958

Synchronicity and Quantum Mechanics

Jung and Pauli agreed that the trinity of classical physics - time, space and causality - could be turned into a quaternity by adding synchronicity as a 4th term.

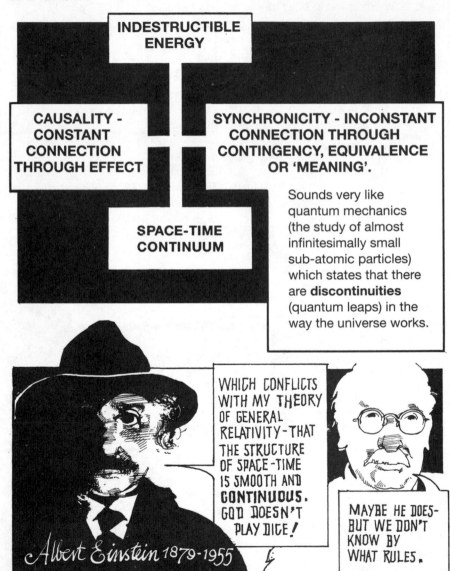

INDESTRUCTIBLE ENERGY

CAUSALITY - CONSTANT CONNECTION THROUGH EFFECT

SYNCHRONICITY - INCONSTANT CONNECTION THROUGH CONTINGENCY, EQUIVALENCE OR 'MEANING'.

SPACE-TIME CONTINUUM

Sounds very like quantum mechanics (the study of almost infinitesimally small sub-atomic particles) which states that there are **discontinuities** (quantum leaps) in the way the universe works.

WHICH CONFLICTS WITH MY THEORY OF GENERAL RELATIVITY - THAT THE STRUCTURE OF SPACE-TIME IS SMOOTH AND **CONTINUOUS.** GOD DOESN'T PLAY DICE!

Albert Einstein 1879-1955

MAYBE HE DOES - BUT WE DON'T KNOW BY WHAT RULES.

An Astrological Experiment

Jung hoped to establish synchronicity as a law equal in status to causality. He tried to make astrology the subject of an experiment that would demonstrate this "law". The basic idea of Jung's experiment was simple.

To see if the "chance" groupings of zodiac figures on a person's horoscope might coincide **meaningfully but acausally** with psychic states and events.

To test for a possible acausal link between psychic **states** and real **events**. For this, Jung chose a specific, measurable event - **marriage**.

Jung devised a carefully planned statistical investigation of the astrological contacts between the birthcharts of a sample number of married couples.

He then asked: What are the specific horoscope configurations that are traditionally said by astrologers to symbolize marriage? There are 3 which all involve the Moon in one person's birthchart being placed in the same zodiacal position (conjunct) as one of the following 3 factors in the partner's birthchart:

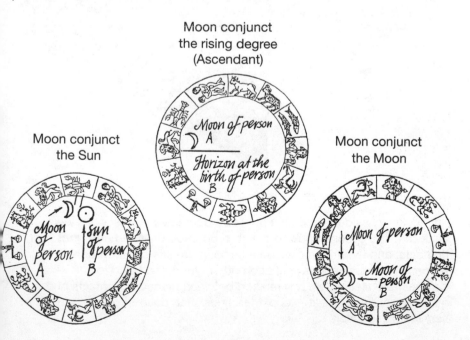

Moon conjunct
the rising degree
(Ascendant)

Moon conjunct
the Sun

Moon conjunct
the Moon

When the first batch of horoscopes arrived, Jung was so impatient for a result that he analyzed it before the rest of the data had been collected. The result showed a strong statistical evidence for a contact of **Moon conjunct Ascendant**. Jung sat in his garden, delighted with the result. But then he saw the face of Mercurius laughing at him in the garden wall.

The trick was evident when the next two batches of horoscopes were analyzed. The second showed a high proportion of **Moon conjunct Sun** contacts; and the third produced significant results of **Moon conjunct Moon**. The results neutralized each other! Jung had failed to demonstrate statistically any relation between planetary contacts and marriage. And yet, the "tricks of Mercurius" had nevertheless produced a very intriguing result!

"Secret Mutual Connivance"

ALL THREE MOON CONTACTS I SET OUT TO FIND ARE CONFIRMED SEPARATELY IN EACH BATCH!

OF COURSE, AS KRAFFT-EBING LONG AGO WARNED YOU...

YOUR OWN **SUBJECTIVE** EXPECTATION IS MIRRORED IN THE MATERIAL!

Jung followed up this recognition with another intriguing experiment.

WHAT HAPPENS IF I CHANGE THE **EXPERIMENTERS?**

Jung chose three individuals whose psychological characters were well-known to him, and asked each one to make a selection of married couples by lot from the horoscope collection.

The first experimenter was in an intense state of emotional turmoil. She selected couples whose predominant contact involved the "excitable" planet Mars.

The second woman was a self-suppressive type who chose couples with contact between the horizon and Moon.

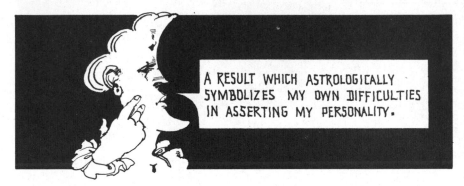

The third woman had strong inner oppositions whose union and reconciliation were her main problem. She chose couples with Sun and Moon conjunctions.

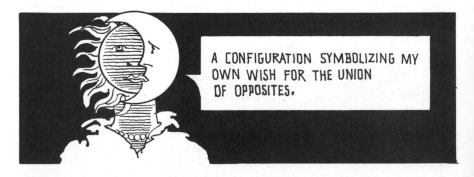

Jung's original experiment had long since parted company with orthodox statistical methods. In searching for an objective law, he had found the reflection of the subjective psyche of the observer in the apparently objective material.

SYNCHRONISTIC EVENTS DRAW THE OBSERVER INTO WHAT IS HAPPENING AND MAKE HIM AN ACCESSORY TO THEM.

What had Jung succeeded to prove? No more than astrologers had always known. "A secret, mutual connivance exists between the material and the psychic state of the astrologer. This correspondence is simply **there** like any other agreeable or annoying incident, and it seems to me doubtful whether it can be proved scientifically to be anything more than that."

The Double Conception

To what real degree is synchronicity either subjective or objective? Or is it partly both?

"Synchronicity takes the coincidence of events in space and time as meaning something more than mere chance, namely, a peculiar interdependence of objective events among themselves **as well as with** the subjective (psychic) states of the observer or observers."

"As well as with?" This is unclear. The relationship between observer and observed remains confused, giving rise to **two** understandings of synchronicity. In one version - Synchronicity I - there is already an "interdependence of objective events amongst themselves" (planets and marriage), observed objectively. Yet the second version - Synchronicity II - involves the **subjective participation** of the observing psyche - the experimenter's psyche is also involved.

Synchronicity I, with its objectivity, could be examined for an inherent theory or law. Synchronicity II, with its **secret, mutual connivance,** was unique and lawless. It depends on, and even brings to light, the psyche of the observing subjects so that the individual's **own** psyche is mysteriously reflected in the objective material.

Jung moves ambiguously between these two versions of synchronicity. If synchronicity in its broadest sense has to be **meaningful,** then it must have a subjective component, because it is impossible to separate "meaning" from subjective psychic activity. Yet in suggesting a form of synchronicity (Synchronicity I) based on an "interdependence of objective events amongst themselves", Jung also has to posit the existence of a psychoid level of reality, existing prior to human consciousness. This implies an order and pattern in the cosmos, a **transcendental meaning** inherent in the collective psyche. Synchronicity postulates a meaning which is a priori to human consciousness and apparently exists outside of man.

Science and the New Age

Jung's synchronicity concept was a major concept in "New Age" thinking in the 60s. Jung was promoted to New Age guru and his ideas were hijacked to justify astrology, the I Ching and other "alternative" practices.

Jung's efforts had contributed to making the study of religion respectable - and the pursuit of religious experience became socially fashionable.

Developments on the leading edge of modern physics - quantum mechanics, the new cosmology, chaos theory - continue to fire the imagination with possible links between physics and the psyche.

THE QUESTION MUST REMAIN OPEN...

THE UNIVERSE HAS NO BEGINNING. IT IS FINITE, BUT WITHOUT BOUNDARY IN SPACE-TIME.

Stephen Hawking

The End?

To the end, Jung went on seeking for "an answer to Job" - a reply to the spiritual dilemma facing modern man. He often retreated to Bollingen to be in the presence of wise old Philemon. Jung himself was now a mythic Philemon, "the sage of Kusnacht".

BUT EVERY LIGHT CASTS A SHADOW ...

Due to the wide range of his thought, Jung's influence extends far wider than the theory and practice of analytical psychology. He bridges the world of science (the testing of theories through empirical, clinical observation) and that of divination (the realm of spirits, omens and mythopoeic imagination).

Jung's critics portray him as a darker figure.

A TYRANNICAL, AMBITIOUS MAN WHO WASTED HIS WIFE'S FORTUNE.

HE TRANSGRESSED ANALYTIC BOUNDARIES AND ENCOURAGED A COURT OF ADORING ACOLYTES.

HE IS INTELLECTUALLY ARROGANT, SUBMERGING EVERYTHING TO HIS OWN THEORIES!

AND HE'S ANTI-SEMITIC!

The accusation of anti-semitism is discussed in the supplement on pages 170-1.

167

Jung's wife Emma died on 27 November 1955. Ruth Bailey, an Englishwoman whom he first met on a trip to East Africa in 1925, became his housekeeper, companion and nurse until his death in 1961.

Carl Gustav Jung

1875   *1961*

Jung continued a vast correspondence about his work and was frequently honoured throughout his old age. At the age of 85, on the last evening of his life, Jung opened and drank one of the best wines in his cellar. He died peacefully the following day, 6 June 1961, in his house on the lake.

A great storm broke across the lake in the hour following his death. The myth of Jung had only just begun.

"From the middle of life onward, only he remains vitally alive who is ready to die with life. For in the secret hour of life's midday the parabola is reversed, death is born. The second half of life does not signify ascent, unfolding, increase, exhuberance, but death, since the end is its goal. The negation of life's fulfilment is synonymous with the refusal to accept its ending. Both mean not wanting to live; not wanting to live is identical with not wanting to die. Waxing and waning making one curve."

The accusation of anti-semitism is discussed in the following Supplement.

SUPPLEMENT

Jung and the Nazis

Accusations of anti-semitism have been made against Jung because of his presidency of the General Medical Society for Psychotherapy at the beginning of the Nazi regime. The Society was originally based in Germany, with an international membership and published a journal, the **Zentralblatt**. In 1933 when the Nazis came to power, the President of the Society was Ernst Kretschmer, and Jung was Vice-President. In June 1933, Kretschmer resigned, realizing that the Society would be forced to conform to Nazi ideology and exclude Jews from membership. Leading members of the Society then urged Jung to become President because he was in a strong position to prevent the Society from being Nazified. As a Swiss, Jung's intellectual and political freedom were not directly threatened by the Nazis.

Jung therefore accepted the Presidency in an attempt to keep psychoanalysis active in Germany and support German analysts, especially Jews. Within months, he formally re-drafted the constitution to make the Society an **international** organization. The new amendments created different national sections. Jung was President of the whole Society as well as of the Swiss section. A German section was founded in Berlin, September 1933, with M.H. Goering as its President, cousin of Nazi Reichsmarschall Hermann Goering. This was the Nazified section of the International Society. However, Jung's amendments allowed membership through **any** national group, which meant that Jewish analysts in Germany could have a platform for their work and preserve their positions by joining the Society through **another** national group.

These constitutional changes were ratified at the Society's congress in May 1934,and Jung declared that the Society should be "neutral as to politics and creed". Nazi persecution eventually made Jung's changes ineffective. Jung finally resigned as President in December 1939 when Germans created and joined other national groups, such as the Hungarian and Japanese, and pressed for them to "conform".

Jung's moves within the Society were not publicly known, he was deeply politically embarrassed by an incident concerning his editorship of the **Zentralblatt.** Goering insisted on a supplement for the German section which declared support for the Fuehrer's ideology. The supplement appeared in the December 1933 issue of the **Zentralblatt** and was distributed internationally. Jung was attacked for supporting a Nazi manifesto in a journal under his editorship, but he claimed that it was distributed without his knowledge or agreement. In 1936, Goering became co-editor, but Jung and his Swiss managing editor, C.A. Meier, continued to publish Jewish authors and review their books, despite Goering's attempts to "conform" the **Zentralblatt.**

After Jung's resignation, Goering in 1940 unconstitutionally declared himself President of the International Society, "conformed" it and its journal, and transferred its headquarters from Zurich to Berlin. In 1940, Jung's writings were suppressed in Germany and his name was put on the black list.

"I Slipped Up"

Aniela Jaffe, Jung's secretary, tells of an incident involving Jung and Leo Baeck (1873-1956), a Rabbi who had been friendly with Jung before the war. Baeck had been a professor of religion in Berlin and had survived the camp at Theresiendstadt. In 1946, he visited Zurich and having heard the accusations of Jung's anti-semitism, he turned down Jung's request to meet. Jung insisted on calling at Baeck's hotel and the two men discussed the anti-semite accusations. Baeck became convinced that they were false and publicly said so, emphasizing a remark by Jung which particularly impressed him - "Well, I slipped up". Baeck's story also convinced another great Jewish scholar, Gershom Scholem, to accept Jung's innocence and attend the Eranos conferences to which he had been invited.

A fuller treatment of Jung, anti-semitism and the Nazis can be found in Aniela Jaffe's **From the Life and Work of C.G. Jung.**

Little Dictionary

Active Imagination: a therapeutic technique which allows unconscious contents to be exposed in a waking state. It is like "dreaming with open eyes", but unlike the passivity of dreams, it demands the active participation of the individual. The images which arise may be elaborated through artistic and self-expressive mediums such as painting.

Amplification: a method of interpretation in which the analyst assists the patient to connect an image in a dream or fantasy with universal imagery. The personal images are amplified by comparison with similar images and motifs found in myths and fairy-tales. By engaging in this process, a synthesis of consciousness and the unconscious, and of personal and collective, is attained. The individual is reconnected with the archetype expressed through the image and the unconscious content is made explicit.

Analytical Psychology: Jung coined this term as early as 1913 to distinguish his approach from Freud's psychoanalysis.

Apports: the paranormal and otherwise inexplicable production or transporting of material objects, as for instance in a seance.

Archetypes: inherited, innate and a priori modes of perception, linked to the instincts, which regulate perception itself. The archetypes are primordial ideas, common to all mankind, and they express only through archetypal images. They are charged with emotion and function autonomously from the unconscious.

Compensation: for Jung, the unconscious stands in a compensatory relationship to consciousnes and functions to restore any imbalance or one-sidedness created by the conscious attitude. Repressed contents re-emerge in dreams, images and symptoms because "every process that goes too far immediately and inevitably calls forth compensation".

Complexes: a collection of images and ideas with a common emotional tone which cluster around an archetypal core. They are autonomous and "behave like independent beings". Complexes are mediated into consciousness by the ego which can be overwhelmed by them (as in psychosis) or identify with them (as in inflation).

Ego: the ego is the centre of the field of consciousness and gives the individual his or her sense of purpose and identity. It organizes the conscious mind, mediating consciousness with the unconscious. The Ego is the precious "light" of consciousness which must always be guarded.

Extrovert & Introvert: the two poles of psychic orientation. In the extrovert attitude, energy flows outwards towards the world and is motivated and oriented by external, objective factors. Introverted energy withdraws from the world and is motivated and oriented by inner, subjective factors.

Functions: Jung distinguished four properties of psychic energy which he terms the four functions, paired in two sets of opposites: thinking-feeling and intuition-sensation. The functions are the means by which we orient ourselves to experience. In any individual, one function is conscious (superior), its opposite is unconscious (inferior) and the remaining two are partially conscious and partially unconscious (auxiliary). The functions combine with the two attitude types (extrovert and introvert), to give eight functional types.

Hysteria: from the Greek for womb, hysteria was once diagnosed as a purely feminine disease. Psychiatry came to use the term to refer to neurotic behaviour in which the physical symptoms, e.g. paralysis or convulsions, derive from psychological rather that physical malfunction. Phobia, or extreme neurotic anxiety, is also a form of hysteria. Jung agrees with Freud that hysterical symptoms are a return of repressed memories in the personal background of the patient, and that they involve misplaced psychic energy, usually sexual. The form of the symptoms is itself symbolic of the nature of the psychological problem.

Individuation: the process of self-development in which an individual integrates the many facets of the psyche to become him or her *self* – an *in*-dividual, a separate, indivisible unity with a sense of psychic wholeness.

Libido: Freud's use of the term libido as "sexual energy" was extended by Jung to include psychic energy in general. He eventually dropped the term libido altogether in favour of "psychic energy" (see psychic energy).

Mandala: Sanskrit for "magic circle". Sacred, geometric paintings used for meditation purposes and characterised by a circle and a square which radiate from a central point. Jung interpreted them as an archetypal expression of the Self and wholeness. Mandala images often emerge in dreams and paintings during analysis.

Mythopoeic Imagination: the myth-making imagination characteristic of primitive mentality but also, according to Jung, of the unconscious. It is to be contrasted with the discursive and directed thought of consciousness. It appears in non-directed fantasy thinking and dream images, and reflects the pre-conscious archetypal structure of the psyche.

Neurosis: originally a "disease of the nerves". Freud saw that this was not a disorder of the nervous system, but of personality, arising from the thwarting of instinctual drives. Beyond the broad distinction between neurosis and psychosis Jung does not attempt a comprehensive classification of neurosis. His analysis took the whole of the disturbed psyche as its subject, and he looked on neurosis as reflecting psychic imbalance. Neurotic symptoms may manifest a compensatory and teleological process of self-healing, since they direct the sufferer's attention to his or her psychic dis-ease.

Projection: the unconscious displacement of psychic contents onto other people or objects. The projected contents may be unacceptable emotions and qualities or they may be beneficial and valuable. Both Shadow and Soul-Image projections are carried by real men and women. The

recollection and integration of projected contents is an important part of analysis and of the individuation process.

Psyche and Psychic Energy: by psyche, Jung means the whole of our being, conscious and unconscious. His analytical psychology attempts to reveal a structure and dynamics of the psyche and to create a typology of psychic energy – attitudes, functions, types and so on. Psychic energy can flow in a number of channels – biological, psychological, spiritual and moral. It will change direction and flow into another channel if it is blocked in any one channel. A shift in the flow of energy has purpose and functions to maintain a balance in the psyche as a whole.

Psychic Reality: a major concept for Jung. The psyche functions in psychic reality. Life is experienced as *psychic reality*, and even "illusory" experiences are real from this point of view. Both the inner and outer world are perceived by us in images, and as evidence of this, we tend to personify unconscious contents. So Christ, for example, is a collective image of the Self and has a real psychic force, quite independent of the historical question of Jesus.

Psychosis: an invasion of consciousness by unconscious contents where the conscious Ego becomes overwhelmed, splitting the individual off from social responses and conventional reality. Consequently, it is difficult for psychotic patients to respond to psychotherapy. The same process that produces madness in one person may be allied to genius in another. Psychotic states can be part of religious conversion and intense inspiration.

Schizophrenia: originally named dementia praecox, it was thought to be a disorder of body chemistry. It is characterised by a splitting apart of thoughts, feelings and actions. Jung acknowledged a physiological component in the illness but considered that its primary origin was psychological – the domination of personality by a split-off complex.

Self: the Self is an image of the unity of the personality as a whole, a central ordering principle. "The self is not only the centre but also the whole circumference which embraces both conscious and unconscious; it is the centre of this totality, just as the ego is the centre of the conscious mind".

Shadow: the inferior, uncivilized and animal qualities repressed by the Ego form a Shadow which stands in compensatory relationship to the "light" of the Ego. The Shadow is "the thing a person has no wish to be". It is of the same sex as the individual and can appear in dreams and fantasies or it can be projected.

Soul Image (anima, animus): an archetypal, inner image of the opposite sex, the anima in a man and the animus in a woman. It appears in dreams and fantasies and is projected onto individuals of the opposite sex, most frequently in the experience of "falling in love". The Soul-Image has a compensatory relationship to the Persona. It functions as a guide to the soul and offers creative possibilities for the individuation process.

Teleology: teleological explanations seek an understanding in terms of purpose and end-goals, rather than a reduction to prior causes. Unlike Freud's psychoanalysis, Jung's analytical psychology frequently refers psychic functioning to such goals, as in the process of individuation.

Transcendent Function: an archetypal process which mediates opposites and enables a transition from one attitude or condition to another. It is activated whenever consciousness is engaged in the tension of opposites. Symbols carry such opposites and thus the transcendent function arises in the attempt to understand the elusive meaning on images and symbols. The function has a healing effect by bridging consciousness and the unconscious and by allowing an individual to move beyond one-sidedness.

Transference: the projection onto the analyst of feelings and ideas which are derived from introjected figures or objects in the patient's past, commonly parental figures. The patient repeats and re-enacts the past relationship with the analyst. The transference may be a positive one (falling in love) or a negative one (hostility and hatred) By analyzing the transference, unconscious patterns become conscious to the patient. **Counter-transference** occurs when the analyst projects his or her own unconscious contents onto the patient.

Unconscious: in analytical psychology, as in psychoanalysis, the existence of the unconscious, with its own laws and functions, is presupposed. It is capable of autonomously affecting and interrupting consciousness. Jung posits both a personal and collective unconscious, both of which stand in compensatory relationship to consciousness. The personal unconscious consists of personal, repressed, infantile contents. The collective unconscious contains collective, inherited contents, the instincts and the archetypes. One of Jung's favourite metaphors for the unconscious is that of the sea. With its fluidity, its calms and storms, mermaids and monsters, it can be a force of either creativity or destruction. Jung considers the unconscious is primarily creative, in the service of the individual.

Unus Mundus: the "One World". This phrase of the alchemists suggests the interpenetration of spirit , soul and matter. As interpreted in Jung's psychology, it describes the inter-relation of psyche and body. With the development of synchronicity, and the positing of a "psychoid substrate" of reality, this metaphor is carried into the inter-relation of psyche and matter. Jung hoped this would lead to a common ground for psychotherapy and physics.

Books by Jung

Jung's Collected Works were originally published by RKP (UK) and the Bollingen Foundation (US). Since 1967, these have been published by Princeton (US) and Bollingen. The following will serve as an accessible introduction to Jung's writings:

Modern Man in Search of a Soul (RKP pbck)

Man and His Symbols (Pan pbck, Jung and others)

Two Essays on Analytical Psychology (CW7, pbck)

Analytical Psychology – The Tavistock Lectures (RKP published 1968, lectures from 1935)

Selected Writings (Ed. Anthony Storr, (Fontana pbck)

The best introduction to Jung is his autobiography, **Memories, Dreams, Reflections**, published posthumously (Fontana pbck). It was recorded and edited by his secretary, Aniela Jaffe, and narrates his story from childhood to old age, serving as the fullest account of the individuation process in the Jungian literature. There is a controversy as to how far it is written in Jung's own words, and how far it has been filtered by Jaffe.

Books about Jung

Recommended biographies are:

Vincent Brome: **Jung, Man and Myth** (Macmillan 1978)

Aniela Jaffe: **From the Life and Work of C.G. Jung** (Hodder & Stoughton 1972)

Laurens van der Post: **Jung and the Story of Our Time** (Penguin 1976)

Introductions to Jung

Henri F. Ellenberger: **The Discovery of the Unconscious** (Basic Books, 1970). It contains a definitive chapter on Jung's work.

Frieda Fordham: **An Introduction to Jung's Psychology** (Pelican originally published 1953).

Jolande Jacobi: **The Psychology of C.G. Jung** (RKP, originally published 1942).

Analytical Psychology

Marie Louise Von Franz has published extensively on Jung and analytical psychology. See especially **C.G. Jung – His Myth in Our Time**. For an introduction to the practice of analytical psychology, see Harry A. Wilmer's illustrated volume **Practical**

Jung; Nuts & Bolts of Jungian Psychotherapy (Chiron 1987). A useful reference to Jungian terminology is **A Critical Dictionary of Jungian Analysis**, Samuels, Shorter & Plaut (RKP 1986).

Jung's ideas have been developed by James Hillman into what he terms Archetypal Psychology. See his **Archetypal Psychology: A brief Account** (Spring pbck 1988) and "Puer Papers" (Ed. Hillman, Spring pbck 1987).

Synchronicity and Divination

Jung's key text is **Synchronicity; An Acausal Connecting Principle** (RKP pbck, also CW8). See also his Foreword to the I Ching (Wilhelm translation, RKP and CW11). Other works include: Marie-Louise von Franz : **On Divination and Synchronicity** (Inner City 1980).

Ira Progoff: **Jung, Synchronicity and Human Destiny** (Dell 1973)

Maggie Hyde : **Jung and Astrology** (Aquarian 1992). This is a specialist book for astrologers.

Maggie Hyde is a writer, lecturer and consultant astrologer born in the North East of England in 1952. After graduating in literature, she was active in the development of a New Philosophy programme for adult education in inner London. Author of **Jung and Astrology** (Aquarian 1992), she is currently Director of the Company of Astrologers, London.

Michael McGuinness is an artist, designer and former art editor at the *Reader's Digest*, the *Sunday Times* and was involved in the award-winning design of the *Independent on Sunday*. He is an Associate Member of the Royal Watercolour Society and has had numerous exhibitions of oils and watercolours. He illustrated the best-selling **Introducing Einstein**.

Index

abreactive recollections 20

alchemy 129–52

anima 93, 94, 96, 98–9

animus 93, 95, 96

Antichrist 126–7

anti-semitism 170–1

archetypal process 62, 63

archetypes 59–63

active imagination 66

astrology 39, 159–63

Burghölzli 24–9

Catholicism 113, 115–16

Charcot, J.-M. 19, 20

Christ 116–17, 122–5

Christianity 124–7, 131

collective unconscious 59, 65, 70, 90, 135

compensation 81

complex 27

death 115

devil 117, 118–19

dissociation 22

dreams 5, 20, 50–1, 59, 70–1

Jung 86, 105

prophetic 104

symbols in 67

dual personality 39–40, 46

ecliptic 120

ego 86–91, 144–6

extroversion 77–8, 82–5

Faust 118–19

female 93, 95, 119

four functions 79–81, 97, 139, 147

Freud, Sigmund 20–1, 26, 32–9

God 6–7, 62, 111, 112, 119

healing function 64–5

I Ching 108–10

incest 46

individuation 112, 136, 140

instinct 59

introversion 77–8, 82–5

intuition 80, 84

irrationality 80

Jung, Carl Gustav

breakdown 47–9

childhood 3–4

criticism of 167

death 168

dreams 86

mid-life crisis 48

mother 10

personalities 10–13

split with Freud 33–9

wife 30, 99

Jungian analysis 63–73

Kant, Immanuel 15

Lapis 130–3, 143

love 97

male 93, 94

Mercurius 135, 138–9

mothers 48

mythology 41, 48

mythopoeic imagination 55

Nazis 170–1

neurosis 74–5, 92

numinous experience 111–12

opposites 121

out-of-body experience 102–3

paranormal 15, 17, 106–10

Pauli, Wolfgang 157–8

Persona, the 91–2, 97

Pisces 120–7

projection 76

psyche defined 76

psychiatry 16–19

psychological types 76–86

psychology

and alchemy 129–52

analytical 74–97

psychosis 25

rationality 80

rebirth 115, 151

relationships 85

religion 4

see also Christ; God

repression 81

schizophrenia 25–6, 36–7, 44

seances 18–19, 23

Self, the 57, 76, 88, 111, 116

sexuality 36–7, 38–9

shadow 86–91, 117, 126, 131

Soul, the 15, 146–7, 150

soul-image 93–7

spirit 75

guide 54, 60

world 9

spiritual issues 21, 43

Spring Point 120–7

Swedenborg, Emanuel 70

symbols 63, 66, 96, 129

synchronicity 158–65

thinking 54, 80–1, 82

time 155–6

transcendent function 65

unconscious, the 19, 22–3, 41–3, 112

Jung's 52–8

structure 76

wholeness 111–15, 150–2

word association 27–9, 32